I0411802

Copyright © 2015 Quote Octopus.com
All rights reserved. No part of this publication may be reproduced, distributed, or transmitted in any form or by any means, including photocopying, recording, or other electronic or mechanical methods, without the prior written permission of the publisher, except in the case of brief quotations embodied in critical reviews and certain other non-commercial uses permitted by copyright law. For permission requests, contact the publisher, addressed "Attention: Permissions Coordinator," at the address below. Quote Octopus 2/53 Barry Street, Melbourne, Victoria, 3053 Australia www.quoteoctopus.com

Get FREE Kindle Books Every Week, Delivered by Email!

Click Here or go to quoteoctopus.com to get your free books!

I have a dream that my four little children will one day live in a nation where they will not be judged by the color of their skin, but by the content of their character.

Martin Luther King, Jr.

Racism is still with us. But it is up to us to prepare our children for what they have to meet, and, hopefully, we shall overcome.

Rosa Parks

All women should know how to take care of children. Most of them will have a husband some day.

Franklin P. Jones

A home with a loving and loyal husband and wife is the supreme setting in which children can be reared in love and righteousness and in which the spiritual and physical needs of children can be met.

David A. Bednar

To be a good father and mother requires that the parents defer many of their own needs and desires in favor of the needs of their children. As a consequence of this sacrifice, conscientious parents develop a nobility of character and learn to put into practice the selfless truths taught by the Savior Himself.

James E. Faust

Freedom is never more than one generation away from extinction. We didn't pass it to our children in the bloodstream. It must be fought for, protected, and handed on for them to do the same.

Ronald Reagan

It is easier to build strong children than to repair broken men.

Frederick Douglass

Children are smarter than any of us. Know how I know that? I don't know one child with a full time job and children.

Bill Hicks

Our world is one of terrible contradictions. Plenty of food, but one billion people go hungry. Lavish lifestyles for a few, but poverty for too many others. Huge advances in medicine while mothers die every day in childbirth, and children die every day from drinking dirty water. Billions spent on weapons to kill people instead of keeping them safe.

Ban Ki-moon

The greatest gifts you can give your children are the roots of responsibility and the wings of independence.

Denis Waitley

The greatest legacy one can pass on to one's children and grandchildren is not money or other material things accumulated in one's life, but rather a legacy of character and faith.

Billy Graham

The natural state of motherhood is unselfishness. When you become a mother, you are no longer the center of your own universe. You relinquish that position to your children.

Jessica Lange

All children are artists. The problem is how to remain an artist once he grows up.

Pablo Picasso

Your children are not your children. They are the sons and daughters of Life's longing for itself. They came through you but not from you and though they are with you yet they belong not to you.

Khalil Gibran

Each day of our lives we make deposits in the memory banks of our children.

Charles R. Swindoll

Security is mostly a superstition. It does not exist in nature, nor do the children of men as a whole experience it. Avoiding danger is no safer in the long run than outright exposure. Life is either a daring adventure, or nothing.

Helen Keller

Regard your soldiers as your children, and they will follow you into the deepest valleys; look on them as your own beloved sons, and they will stand by you even unto death.

Sun Tzu

When you have a godly husband, a godly wife, children who respect their parents and who are loved by their parents, who provide for those children their physical and spiritual and material needs, lovingly, you have the ideal unit.

Jerry Falwell

Keep me away from the wisdom which does not cry, the philosophy which does not laugh and the greatness which does not bow before children.

Khalil Gibran

The depth of the love of parents for their children cannot be measured. It is like no other relationship. It exceeds concern for life itself. The love of a parent for a child is continuous and transcends heartbreak and disappointment.

James E. Faust

Children should be able to live a life free from bullying and harassment and it is time that we all took a stand against this.

Katherine Jenkins

Adults are just outdated children.

Dr. Seuss

The greatest sign of success for a teacher... is to be able to say, 'The children are now working as if I did not exist.'

Maria Montessori

Live so that when your children think of fairness, caring, and integrity, they think of you.

H. Jackson Brown, Jr.

Without education, your children can never really meet the challenges they will face. So it's very important to give children education and explain that they should play a role for their country.

Nelson Mandela

I believe our legacy will be defined by the accomplishments and fearless nature by which our daughters and sons take on the global challenges we face. I also wonder if perhaps the most lasting expression of one's humility lies in our ability to foster and mentor our children.

Naveen Jain

Because of my childhood where I was constantly by myself, I always feel lonely. I have a lot of people that I absolutely love and I know love me but I can't get rid of that feeling of loneliness no matter who I'm with - even with my children.

Natalia Vodianova

I think America's food culture is embedded in fast-food culture. And the real question that we have is: How are we going to teach slow-food values in a fast-food world? Of course, it's very, very difficult to do, especially when children have grown up eating fast food and the values that go with that.

Alice Waters

Real fatherhood means love and commitment and sacrifice and a willingness to share responsibility and not walking away from one's children.

William Bennett

As you may know, some of the stereotyped behaviors exhibited by autistic children are also found in zoo animals who are raised in a barren environment.

Temple Grandin

Creativity is not just for artists. It's for businesspeople looking for a new way to close a sale; it's for engineers trying to solve a problem; it's for parents who want their children to see the world in more than one way.

Twyla Tharp

There is nothing funny about Halloween. This sarcastic festival reflects, rather, an infernal demand for revenge by children on the adult world.

Jean Baudrillard

The idea of kids helping other kids is such a great way to

introduce children to being involved in charitable causes and volunteer work, setting them on the path to doing good for others throughout their lives.

Brandy Norwood

It's a funny feeling to work with people who you consider your colleagues and to realize that they actually are young enough to be your children.

Alan Alda

Little children are still the symbol of the eternal marriage between love and duty.

George Eliot

I believe the best service to the child is the service closest to the child, and children who are victims of neglect, abuse, or abandonment must not also be victims of bureaucracy. They deserve our devoted attention, not our divided attention.

Kenny Guinn

It's important to give a better country to your children, but it is more important to give better children to your country.

Carlos Slim

Now the problem with standardized tests is that it's based on the mistake that we can simply scale up the education of children like you would scale up making carburetors. And we can't, because human beings are very different from motorcars, and they have feelings about what they do and motivations in doing it, or not.

Ken Robinson

We are raising today's children in sterile, risk-averse and highly structured environments. In so doing, we are failing to cultivate artists, pioneers and entrepreneurs, and instead cultivating a generation of children who can follow the rules in organized sports games, sit for hours in front of screens and mark bubbles on standardized tests.

Darell Hammond

For in the final analysis, our most basic common link is that we all inhabit this small planet. We all breathe the same air. We all cherish our children's futures. And we are all mortal.

John F. Kennedy

It is a masterpiece of the devil to make us believe that children cannot understand religion. Would Christ have made a child the standard of faith if He had known that it was not capable of understanding His words?

Dwight L. Moody

A treatment method or an educational method that will work for one child may not work for another child. The one common denominator for all of the young children is that early intervention does work, and it seems to improve the prognosis.

Temple Grandin

If help and salvation are to come, they can only come from the children, for the children are the makers of men.

Maria Montessori

The one thing I want to leave my children is an honorable name.

Theodore Roosevelt

Well, we lost a lot of our independence already. We are dependent on China for credit. We are dependent on Middle Eastern countries for energy supplies. And many Americans are dependent on the government for their income, health care, education of their children, food stamps.

Jim DeMint

Education promotes equality and lifts people out of poverty. It teaches children how to become good citizens. Education is not just for a privileged few, it is for everyone. It is a fundamental human right.

Ban Ki-moon

Lucky that man whose children make his happiness in life and not his grief, the anguished disappointment of his hopes.

Euripides

I tell myself that God gave my children many gifts - spirit, beauty, intelligence, the capacity to make friends and to inspire respect. There was only one gift he held back - length of life.

Rose Kennedy

There are over 200 million illiterate women in India. This low literacy negatively impacts not just their lives but also their families' and the country's economic development. A girl's lack of education also has a negative impact on the health and well-being of her children.

Sachin Tendulkar

I think that enduring, committed love between a married couple, along with raising children, is the most noble act anyone can aspire to. It is not written about very much.

Nicholas Sparks

Among the other values children should be taught are respect for others, beginning with the child's own parents and family; respect for the symbols of faith and the patriotic beliefs of others; respect for law and order; respect for the property of others; respect for authority.

James E. Faust

My wife, a schoolteacher, very disciplined. If you think I'm tough, trust me, and wait till you see when the children are on the naughty step. It's hilarious. So we decided that I'm going to work like a donkey and provide amazing support for the family.

Gordon Ramsay

The human overpopulation issue is the topic I see as the most vital to solve if our children and grandchildren are to have a good quality of life.

Alexandra Paul

The best inheritance a parent can give his children is a few minutes of his time each day.

Orlando Aloysius Battista

Grown-ups never understand anything for themselves, and it is tiresome for children to be always and forever explaining things to them.

Antoine de Saint-Exupery

We have a responsibility as a state to protect our most vulnerable citizens: our children, seniors, people with disabilities. That is our moral obligation. But there is an economic justification too - we all pay when the basic needs of our citizens are unmet.

John Lynch

God put us here to prepare this place for the next generation. That's our job. Raising children and helping the community, that's preparing for the next generation.

Dikembe Mutombo

We are all equal children before our mother; and India asks each one of us, in whatsoever role we play in the complex drama of nation-building, to do our duty with integrity, commitment and unflinching loyalty to the values enshrined in our Constitution.

Pranab Mukherjee

My father's best friend, Georgie Terra, was an Italian guy. The children and the cousins and nieces and nephews were children of the Mafia. Those were the children he grew up with. If you want to go to a safe neighborhood, go to where the Mafia is.

Louis Gossett, Jr.

In giving us children, God places us in a position of both leadership and service. He calls us to give up our lives for someone else's sake - to abandon our own desires and put our child's interests first. Yet, according to His perfect design, it is through this selflessness that we can become truly fulfilled.

Charles Stanley

Love exercised while duty is neglected will make children headstrong, willful, perverse, selfish, and disobedient. If stern duty is left to stand alone without love to soften and win, it will have a similar result. Duty and love must be blended in order that children may be properly disciplined.

Ellen G. White

The war on terror is the most insane and immoral war of all time. The Americans are doing what they did in Vietnam, bombing villages. But how can a civilised nation do this? How can you can eliminate suspects, their wives, their children, their families, their neighbours? How can you justify this?

Imran Khan

I have led an unusual life. I have buried a father killed at age 50 and two brothers killed in the prime of their lives. I raised my children as a single mother when my husband was arrested and held for eight years without a conviction -

a hostage to my political career.

Benazir Bhutto

The culture is going into a psychological depression. We are concerned about our place in the world, about being competitive: Will my children have as much as I have? Will I ever own my own home? How can I pay for a new car? Are immigrants taking away my white world?

James Hillman

Modern cynics and skeptics... see no harm in paying those to whom they entrust the minds of their children a smaller wage than is paid to those to whom they entrust the care of their plumbing.

John F. Kennedy

A family is a unit composed not only of children but of men, women, an occasional animal, and the common cold.

Ogden Nash

I have to get a licence to drive a motorcycle to protect myself and the people around me. I am adamant there should be some sort of licensing required to have children.

Tim Allen

When you truly accept that those children in some far off place in the global village have the same value as you in God's eyes or even in just your eyes, then your life is forever changed; you see something that you can't un-see.

Bono

I'm a man with many defects. I love. I sing. I dream. I was born in the poor countryside. I was raised in the countryside, planting corn and selling sweets made by my grandmother. My children, my two daughters are with me and I want a better world for my grandchildren, for your grandchildren.

Hugo Chavez

Some people have told me that I'm grumpy; it's not something that I'm aware of. It's not like I walk around poking children in the eye... not very small ones, anyway.

Dylan Moran

Since the beginning of time, children have not liked to study. They would much rather play, and if you have their interests at heart, you will let them learn while they play; they will find that what they have mastered is child's play.

Carl Orff

When I hear people talk about juggling, or the sacrifices they make for their children, I look at them like they're crazy, because 'sacrifice' infers that there was something better to do than being with your children.

Chris Rock

Nothing you do for children is ever wasted. They seem not to notice us, hovering, averting our eyes, and they seldom offer thanks, but what we do for them is never wasted.

Garrison Keillor

The direct use of force is such a poor solution to any problem, it is generally employed only by small children and large nations.

David Friedman

Perhaps the soundest advice for parents is: Lighten up. People have been raising children for approximately as long as there have been people.

George Will

Cooking with your kids and engaging them in hands-on activities are two ways to begin to educate children about the healthy eating, and kick start the important task to help change how the younger generation looks at food and nutrition.

Marcus Samuelsson

What is missing from today's dialogue is the effect autism is having on families, our society and what the unknown factors are. The 300lb. gorilla in the room is that our children with autism today will soon become adults with autism.

Jenny McCarthy

Men, women, and children who cannot live on gravity alone need something to satisfy their gayer, lighter moods and hours, and he who ministers to this want is, in my opinion, in a business established by the Creator of our nature. If he worthily fulfills his mission and amuses without corrupting, he need never feel that he has lived in vain.

P. T. Barnum

I have no regrets about not having children. I still wait for the pang of guilt, but I have none. I tune into the television show 'Nanny 911' occasionally which reminds me how much patience and love it take to be a good parent.

Amanda Donohoe

Listen to the desires of your children. Encourage them and then give them the autonomy to make their own decision.

Denis Waitley

Women's liberation is just a lot of foolishness. It's men who are discriminated against. They can't bear children. And no one is likely to do anything about that.

Golda Meir

Ensuring a bright future for all our children is the responsibility of the community, the schools, families and like it or not- politicians as well.

Michael N. Castle

My books are about ordinary people, like you, me, people on the street, people who really have an expectation of reasonable happiness in life, want their life to have a sense of security and predictability, who want to belong to something bigger than them, who want love and affection in their life, who want a good future for the children.

Khaled Hosseini

Courage: Great Russian word, fit for the songs of our children's children, pure on their tongues, and free.

Anna Akhmatova

It's hard to think it's important to try out as cheerleader when you're starring on Broadway. But you do kind of miss the things that I now see my children doing. I'm just happy they are not actors. The Valentine's Day dance is really important. Pitching in Little League is very important. And the medals and the scouts are really important.

Bonnie Bedelia

Oh, what a tangled web do parents weave when they think that their children are naive.

Ogden Nash

One thing that I noticed is having met some former Taliban is even they, as children, grew up being indoctrinated. They grew up in violence. They grew up in war. They were taught to hate. They were, they grew up in very ignorant cultures where they didn't learn about the outside world.

Greg Mortenson

Let me tell you that the children from their very birth are born to evil. Satan seems to have control of them. He seems to take possession of their young minds, and they are corrupted. Why do fathers and mothers act as though a lethargy was upon them? They do not mistrust that Satan is sowing evil seed in their families.

Ellen G. White

Let us put our minds together and see what life we can make for our children.

Sitting Bull

A vegetarian is a person who won't eat anything that can have children.

David Brenner

Looking ahead, future generations may learn their social skills from robots in the first place. The cute yellow Keepon robot from Carnegie Mellon University has shown the ability to facilitate social interactions with autistic children. Morphy at the University of Washington happily teaches gestures to children by demonstration.

Daniel H. Wilson

When motherhood becomes the fruit of a deep yearning, not the result of ignorance or accident, its children will become the foundation of a new race.

Margaret Sanger

Learning a foreign language, and the culture that goes with it, is one of the most useful things we can do to broaden the empathy and imaginative sympathy and cultural outlook of children.

Michael Gove

As children, our imaginations are vibrant, and our hearts are open. We believe that the bad guy always loses and that the tooth fairy sneaks into our rooms at night to put money under our pillow. Everything amazes us, and we think anything is possible. We continuously experience life with a sense of newness and unbridled curiosity.

Yehuda Berg

Always kiss your children goodnight, even if they're already asleep.

H. Jackson Brown, Jr.

We must ensure that while eliminating child labor in the export industry, we are also eliminating their labour from the informal sector, which is more invisible to public scrutiny - and thus leaves the children more open to abuse and exploitation.

Carol Bellamy

Those who educate children well are more to be honored than they who produce them; for these only gave them life, those the art of living well.

Aristotle

The ultimate test of a moral society is the kind of world that it leaves to its children.

Dietrich Bonhoeffer

Parenting classes should be mandatory, whether you are adopting or not, and would include an evaluation of your current physical, mental and financial state as well as how ready you are to take on the rigors of parenthood. Our children are our most precious natural resource, and there is absolutely no other way to parent but to put them first.

Dale Archer

I've always assumed that my parents and my in-laws would live with me when I get older and have children. I just assume it will happen and that it's the right way to do things. It's a deeply Indian custom - that you kind of inherit your parents and your spouse's parents and you take care of them eventually.

Mindy Kaling

And I remember going to the record studio and there was a park across the street and I'd see all the children playing and I would cry because it would make me sad that I would have to work instead.

Michael Jackson

Children are supposed to help hold a marriage together. They do this in a number of ways. For instance, they demand so much attention that a husband and wife, concentrating on their children, fail to notice each other's faults.

Richard Armour

Back in my days as a children's book editor, my superiors caught on to the fact that teenagers were using the Internet to gossip about each other, and thought it might be nifty to develop a series of books about an anonymous high-school blogger who gossips about her classmates. The concept was passed on to me.

Cecily von Ziegesar

Of course as children, we all, in all cultures and societies, learn behavior from observation, imitation, and encouragement of various kinds. So by the suggestion made, we all 'pretend' most of the time.

Gary Gygax

We spend the first twelve months of our children's lives teaching them to walk and talk and the next twelve telling them to sit down and shut up.

Phyllis Diller

I like children - fried.

W. C. Fields

We are now at a point where we must educate our children in what no one knew yesterday, and prepare our schools for what no one knows yet.

Margaret Mead

Mama exhorted her children at every opportunity to 'jump at the sun.' We might not land on the sun, but at least we would get off the ground.

Zora Neale Hurston

I say the law should be blind to race, gender and sexual orientation, just as it claims to be blind to wealth and power. There should be no specially protected groups of any kind, except for children, the severely disabled and the elderly, whose physical frailty demands society's care.

Camille Paglia

We've got to work to save our children and do it with full respect for the fact that if we do not, no one else is going to do it.

Dorothy Height

I hold that the beginning of modern Irish drama was in the winter of 1898, at a school feast at Coole, when Douglas Hyde and Miss Norma Borthwick acted in Irish in a Punch and Judy show; and the delighted children went back to tell their parents what grand curses 'An Craoibhin' had put on the baby and the policeman.

Lady Gregory

Mothers are fonder than fathers of their children because they are more certain they are their own.

Aristotle

Children that have been petted and waited upon, always expect it; and if their expectations are not met, they are disappointed and discouraged. This same disposition will be seen through their whole lives, and they will be helpless, leaning upon others for aid, expecting others to favor them and yield to them.

Ellen G. White

There can be no equality or opportunity if men and women and children be not shielded in their lives from the consequences of great industrial and social processes which they cannot alter, control, or singly cope with.

Woodrow Wilson

I am afraid we must make the world honest before we can honestly say to our children that honesty is the best policy.

George Bernard Shaw

Recommend virtue to your children; it alone, not money, can make them happy. I speak from experience.

Ludwig van Beethoven

The Son of God became incarnate in the souls of men to instill the feeling of brotherhood. All are brothers and all children of God.

Pope Francis

Well, you don't get to do things that other children get to do, having friends and slumber parties and buddies. There were none of that for me. I didn't have friends when I was little. My brothers were my friends.

Michael Jackson

Raising children is a creative endeavor, an art rather than a science.

Bruno Bettelheim

Sometimes I think God loves the ones who most desperately ache and are most desperately lost - his or her wildest, most messed-up children - the way you'd ache and love a screwed-up rebel daughter in juvenile hall.

Anne Lamott

Asking questions is what brains were born to do, at least when we were young children. For young children, quite literally, seeking explanations is as deeply rooted a drive as seeking food or water.

Alison Gopnik

Strip the proud nobility of their bloated estates, reduce them to a level with plain republicans, send forth to labor, and teach their children to enter the workshops or handle the plow, and you will thus humble proud traitors.

Thaddeus Stevens

Tell the children the truth.

Bob Marley

Children are educated by what the grown-up is and not by his talk.

Carl Jung

If you must hold yourself up to your children as an object lesson, hold yourself up as a warning and not as an example.

George Bernard Shaw

Most American children suffer too much mother and too little father.

Gloria Steinem

God is not upset that Gandhi was not a Christian, because God is not a Christian! All of God's children and their different faiths help us to realize the immensity of God.

Desmond Tutu

Mothers always find ways to fit in the work - but then when you're working, you feel that you should be spending time with your children and then when you're with your children, you're thinking about working.

Alice Hoffman

Showing young children in these communities, that there are outlets for their feelings, that there is room in a space for their stories to be told, and that they will be applauded - and it's not about ego, it's about connection: that their pain is everybody else's pain.

Tom Hiddleston

A nation that does not stand for its children does not stand for anything and will not stand tall in the future.

Marian Wright Edelman

The government has convinced parents that at some point it's no longer their responsibility. And in fact, they force them, in many respects, to turn their children over to the public education system and wrest control from them and block them out of participation of that. That has to change or education will not improve in this country.

Rick Santorum

For some students, school is the only place where they get a hot meal and a warm hug. Teachers are sometimes the only ones who tell our children they can go from an Indian reservation to the Ivy League, from the home of a struggling single mom to the White House.

Denise Juneau

Even if you can't afford to travel the world, you can take your children to the museum, zoo or local park. And don't be afraid to take them to grown-up spots. Eating out in a restaurant teaches children how to be quiet and polite and gives them the pleasure of knowing you trust them to behave.

Kimora Lee Simmons

We need to teach the next generation of children from day one that they are responsible for their lives. Mankind's greatest gift, also its greatest curse, is that we have free choice. We can make our choices built from love or from fear.

Elisabeth Kubler-Ross

Always be nice to your children because they are the ones who will choose your rest home.

Phyllis Diller

Children are not unforgiving. You can punish them and they will hug you in a few minutes.

T. D. Jakes

I was shortly again at the castle, and the Princess gave me her hand to kiss and then brought her children, the young princes and princesses, and we played together, as if we had known each other for years.

Max Muller

A man builds a house in England with the expectation of living in it and leaving it to his children; we shed our houses in America as easily as a snail does his shell.

Harriet Beecher Stowe

Studies show that children best flourish when one mom and one dad are there to raise them.

John Boehner

I'm not particularly a feminist, but if you get women off the animal cycle of reproduction and give them some say in how many children they'll have, immediately the floor will rise.

Christopher Hitchens

As a parent, I can empathize with how difficult raising children can be. There are challenges, especially within the framework of divorce, when parental guilt can sometimes blur what should be the best decision.

LZ Granderson

I wouldn't want to go back over my life. I've done it all. I wouldn't have wanted to miss the Marine Corps. I wouldn't have wanted to miss the war. I wouldn't have missed college. Or playin' for the Colts. I got all the money I need. Five children. I got a truck. I have no regrets whatsoever.

Art Donovan

We beg you to save young America from the blight of race prejudice. Do not bind the children within the narrow circles of your own lives.

Charles Hamilton Houston

People are going to be living quite soon for 100 years. Our idea of how a family works no longer applies. It's no good saying you're going to have children for 15 years and then you're going to retire and have hobbies, because you've got 40 more years to go after 60 and you're in good health until 90 or something.

Theodore Zeldin

The most important thing a father can do for his children is to love their mother.

Theodore Hesburgh

The whole commerce between master and slave is a perpetual exercise of the most boisterous passions, the most unremitting despotism on the one part, and degrading submissions on the other. Our children see this, and learn to imitate it.

Thomas Jefferson

We must respect the other fellow's religion, but only in the sense and to the extent that we respect his theory that his wife is beautiful and his children smart.

H. L. Mencken

Children will not remember you for the material things you provided but for the feeling that you cherished them.

Richard L. Evans

For Jesus, there are no countries to be conquered, no ideologies to be imposed, no people to be dominated. There are only children, women and men to be loved.

Henri Nouwen

I have a feeling that being in love sometimes means the projection of your desires onto another person. The important thing is that you like the other person, respect the other person and want to raise children with the other person.

Eric Braeden

Children are natural Zen masters; their world is brand new in each and every moment.

John Bradshaw

If you're sitting in your minivan, playing your computer animated films for your children in the back seat, is it the animation that's entertaining you as you drive and listen? No, it's the storytelling. That's why we put so much importance on story. No amount of great animation will save a bad story.

John Lasseter

Morality becomes hypocrisy if it means accepting mothers' suffering or dying in connection with unwanted pregnancies and illegal abortions and unwanted children.

Gro Harlem Brundtland

We all had lots of stories of our sad experiences - they mourned the death of my wife with me - but we were hopeful that the children would return.

Otto Frank

Whether it's making sure that families have access to quality health care and child care, or making sure that our children receive the best educational opportunities we can give them, we must remain committed to these needs because our children are our future.

Blanche Lincoln

Many immigrants do not talk about what they endured back home. They were fleeing that world, and when they left they didn't want to talk about it because there had been pain and heartbreak under the caste system of the South. They didn't want to burden their children with what they had endured.

Isabel Wilkerson

Mother is the name for God in the lips and hearts of little children.

William Makepeace Thackeray

For unflagging interest and enjoyment, a household of children, if things go reasonably well, certainly all other forms of success and achievement lose their importance by comparison.

Theodore Roosevelt

I take a very practical view of raising children. I put a sign in each of their rooms: 'Checkout Time is 18 years.'

Erma Bombeck

If Jesus had been killed twenty years ago, Catholic school children would be wearing little electric chairs around their necks instead of crosses.

Lenny Bruce

This is the moment when we must come together to save this planet. Let us resolve that we will not leave our children a world where the oceans rise and famine spreads and terrible storms devastate our lands.

Barack Obama

Few things are more satisfying than seeing your children have teenagers of their own.

Doug Larson

Parents were invented to make children happy by giving them something to ignore.

Ogden Nash

The conscience of children is formed by the influences that surround them; their notions of good and evil are the result of the moral atmosphere they breathe.

Jean Paul

We need to decide that we will not go to war, whatever reason is conjured up by the politicians or the media, because war in our time is always indiscriminate, a war against innocents, a war against children.

Howard Zinn

But we're born as children and we look at the world with open eyes... And we don't judge and we don't betray. We're

not jealous. We're not envious. We're not even weary,
which is a danger also as kids. They have to learn a certain
amount of awareness.

Colin Farrell

Can we really believe that we are living a good life, an
ethically decent life if we don't do anything serious to help
reduce poverty around the world and help save the lives of
children or adults who are likely to die if we don't increase
the amount of aid we are giving.

Peter Singer

Women hold up more than half the sky and represent much
of the world's unrealized potential. They are the educators.
They raise the children. They hold families together and
increasingly drive economies. They are natural leaders. We
need their full engagement... in government, business and
civil society.

Ban Ki-moon

The minimum wage is not something that you want to stay
on as a permanent basis. For example, if you have a
minimum wage job, you don't stay there 20 or 30 years.
You don't put your children through college working on
minimum wage.

John Raese

One must ask children and birds how cherries and strawberries taste.

Johann Wolfgang von Goethe

If you ask the government to solve all of your problems, it's a bit like asking your wife to cook and clean, to raise the children, to hold down a second job to help with the family finances, to keep her parents happy and well and keep your parents happy and well, and to also - to do the lawn and clean the gutters.

P. J. O'Rourke

I would have liked having children to some degree, but frankly I haven't got the time to take the kids to the goddamn ballgame.

Albert Ellis

The parents have a right to say that no teacher paid by their money shall rob their children of faith in God and send them back to their homes skeptical, or infidels, or agnostics, or atheists.

William Jennings Bryan

We are all dreamers creating the next world, the next beautiful world for ourselves and for our children.

Yoko Ono

Build traditions of family vacations and trips and outings. These memories will never be forgotten by your children.

Ezra Taft Benson

I want to get married and have children and live happily ever after. That's important to me.

Cory Monteith

Having children is life-changing, to state the obvious. It's a gigantic shift in your life and I welcomed it.

Thandie Newton

Many low-income children face chronic stress from nutritional deprivation or persistent violence at home or in the community. By addressing their medical, emotional and developmental needs through a comprehensive clinical care model, we can lower their risk of developing long-term physical and mental health issues.

Irwin Redlener

The World War I, I'm a child of World War I. And I really know about the children of war. Because both my parents were both badly damaged by the war. My father, physically, and both mentally and emotionally. So, I know exactly what it's like to be brought up in an atmosphere of a continual harping on the war.

Doris Lessing

The abundance of cheap food with low nutritional value in the Western diet has wreaked havoc on our health; in America, one third of children and two thirds of adults are overweight or obese and are more likely to develop diabetes and cardiovascular disease.

Ellen Gustafson

I think we put our children at an enormous disadvantage by not educating them in war, by not letting them understand about it at an early age.

Suzanne Collins

What I find problematic is the suggestion that when, say, Madonna adopts an African child, she is saving Africa. It's not that simple. You have to do more than go there and adopt a child or show us pictures of children with flies in their eyes. That simplifies Africa.

Chimamanda Ngozi Adichie

The sexual abuse and exploitation of children is one of the most vicious crimes conceivable, a violation of mankind's most basic duty to protect the innocent.

James T. Walsh

If American women would increase their voting turnout by ten percent, I think we would see an end to all of the budget cuts in programs benefiting women and children.

Coretta Scott King

Do all children have some inherent right to live in America if they have done nothing wrong? If not, then why should the children of illegal immigrants have such a right?

Thomas Sowell

I wish people would realize that animals are totally dependent on us, helpless, like children, a trust that is put upon us.

James Herriot

I have often thought what a melancholy world this would be without children, and what an inhuman world without the aged.

Samuel Taylor Coleridge

After I won the Oscar, my salary doubled, my friends tripled, my children became more popular at school, my butcher made a pass at me, and my maid hit me up for a raise.

Shirley Jones

As a young man, I saw families prosper without reading because there were always sufficient opportunities for willing workers who could follow simple instructions. This is no longer the case. Children who don't read are, in the main, destined for lesser lives. I feel a deep sense of responsibility to change this.

Walter Dean Myers

Education makes children less dependent upon others and opens doors to better jobs and career possibilities.

Solomon Ortiz

People say, When you have children, everything changes. But maybe things are awakened that were already there.

Meryl Streep

I believe we should spend less time worrying about the quantity of books children read and more time introducing them to quality books that will turn them on to the joy of reading and turn them into lifelong readers.

James Patterson

The hardest thing about my job isn't the snake bites or the crocodiles, it's being away from my children. I have a really religious satellite phone call every day back to the boys, wherever we are, whatever time zone, to say goodnight.

Bear Grylls

At the end of the day, I got to live my life for my family, for my children, and I'm going to do what's best for them.

T.I.

What has made America amazing has been the fact that throughout our history, throughout the more than 200 years of our history, there have been men and women of courage who stood up and decided it was more important to look out for the future of their children and their grandchildren than their own political futures.

Scott Walker

Stuttering is painful. In Sunday school, I'd try to read my lessons, and the children behind me were falling on the floor with laughter.

James Earl Jones

Our children are obese, either have or being threatened by diabetes, high blood pressure, high cholesterol, and not socially adjusting properly to others because of a lack of fitness.

Richard Simmons

Children are extremely perceptive and absorb what goes on around them long before they can talk or even comprehend language. They are like finely tuned receivers that pick up much more than is merely said. They are receptive and attuned to every mood, feeling, and change that goes on in people around them.

Theodore Isaac Rubin

Childhood depression tends to be more common in inner cities, being most frequently related to serious social deprivation, bullying, domestic violence, wartime experience and famine. It is, for example, a serious problem among children who are traumatised refugees.

Robert Winston

I was thinking that when I have children, that I should always dress as a character for them, so they think their mom is Alice in Wonderland or Cinderella. It would be totally messed up!

Gwen Stefani

Our children can achieve great things when we set high expectations for them.

Jeb Bush

People have come to me for my opinion since 'October Baby.' But, hey, look, I'm an actor who is very fortunate to be in a movie that's making wonderful noise, and hopefully helping parents and children to be a little closer. Leave me alone. I'm not talking about politics. I'm just trying to have a conversation with my own kids.

John Schneider

The things that make me happiest in the whole world are going on the occasional picnic, either with my children or with my partner; big family gatherings; and being able to go to the grocery store - if I can get those things in, I'm doing good.

Kate Winslet

Create a garden; bring children to farms for field trips. I think it's important that parents and teachers get together to do one or two things they can accomplish well - a teaching garden, connecting with farms nearby, weave food into the curriculum.

Alice Waters

Having children made us look differently at all these things that we take for granted, like taking your child to get a vaccine against measles or polio.

Melinda Gates

I have never experienced being madly in love the way most people seem to have been, although it is not something I would miss. Instead I have had an enormous ability to love my children and my grandchildren and my great grandchildren.

Astrid Lindgren

For most women, including women who want to have children, contraception is not an option; it is a basic health care necessity.

Louise Slaughter

Anyone who is interested in the psychology of children will have observed that whereas one child will resist temptation or seduction, another will easily yield to it. There are children who will hardly oppose any resistance to the invitation of an unknown person to follow him; others who react in an opposite way in the same circumstances.

Karl Abraham

Children who are treated as if they are uneducable almost invariably become uneducable.

Kenneth Clark

Our most basic common link is that we all inhabit this planet. We all breathe the same air. We all cherish our children's future. And we are all mortal.

John F. Kennedy

The most important thing that parents can teach their children is how to get along without them.

Frank A. Clark

Parentage is a very important profession, but no test of fitness for it is ever imposed in the interest of the children.

George Bernard Shaw

No man should bring children into the world who is unwilling to persevere to the end in their nature and education.

Plato

What white man has ever seen me drunk? Who has ever come to me hungry and left me unfed? Who has seen me beat my wives or abuse my children? What law have I broken?

Sitting Bull

My mother said, Don't worry abot what people think now. Think about whether your children and grandchildren will think you've done well.

Lord Mountbatten

While I've spent a lot of quality time with my children, perhaps it's not been enough.

Jesse Jackson

Very gifted people, they win and they win, and they are told that they win because they are a winner. That seems like a positive thing to tell children, but ultimately, what that means is when they lose, it must make them a loser.

Joshua Waitzkin

I've got four lovely children, ten lovely grandchildren, and I left parliament to devote more time to politics, and I think that what is really going on in Britain is a growing sense of alienation. People don't feel anyone listens to them.

Tony Benn

I feel very blessed to have two wonderful, healthy children who keep me completely grounded, sane and throw up on my shoes just before I go to an awards show just so I know to keep it real.

Reese Witherspoon

Raising children is an enormously important part of life. I think one of the most important, or the most important, period.

Eric Braeden

When men or women make their work their top priority and become hostile to the normal, natural needs of their children and spouse - obviously, something is wrong.

Laura Schlessinger

The only defense is offense, which means that you have to kill more women and children more quickly than the enemy if you wish to save yourselves.

Stanley Baldwin

Everything I thought I'd hate about having children - the crying, the screaming - nothing fazes me. I love it all, and it's relaxed me.

Elton John

Can you believe approximately 17 percent of American children ages 2 to 19 years are obese? How about this fact: approximately 60 percent of overweight children ages 5 to 10 already have at least one risk factor for heart disease? We are all to blame for this - parents, schools, kids - all of us.

Alison Sweeney

Why in almost all societies have married women specialized in bearing and rearing children and in certain agricultural activities, whereas married men have done most of the fighting and market work?

Gary Becker

One of the problems we have is children are not in school long enough in the day and during the year.

Michael Gove

We must do everything in our power to keep families together, and to use common sense in our immigration laws. Children deserve better than to lose a parent because of an inflexible law.

Jose Serrano

It's a failure of national vision when you regard children as weapons, and talents as materials you can mine, assay, and fabricate for profit and defense.

John Hersey

Familiarity breeds contempt - and children.

Mark Twain

My mother loved children - she would have given anything

if I had been one.

Groucho Marx

I have two young children with autism. What could they have ever done to deserve that? What kind of a God allows the innocent to suffer? It's a mystery. Yet still, I believe in God.

Fred Melamed

The idea that children are passive repositories to be shaped by their parents has been massively overstated. A child's peer group is a far greater determinant of its development and achievements than parental aspiration.

Steven Pinker

We pay a price when we deprive children of the exposure to the values, principles, and education they need to make them good citizens.

Sandra Day O'Connor

A lesser complaint: hair extensions. There are moments on 'All My Children' when half the women actors, young and old, seem to be afflicted by android Barbie creep. All those thick swatches of lifeless strands clustering lankly round ladies' necks! Like orange tanning spray, this is a fashion fad that should be put out of its misery.

Camille Paglia

Children see things very well sometimes - and idealists even better.

Lorraine Hansberry

God has given His children a love that is so great in Christ that the world can't touch it with chocolates, roses, or diamonds.

Monica Johnson

I don't have friends, I have thousands of acquaintances. No friends. I figured I had a wife and children.

Charles Bronson

I call upon my God to judge me, he knows that I love my friends and above all others my wife and children, the, oppinion of the world to contrary notwithstanding.

Stand Watie

As a free-speech advocate, I believe that adults should have access to any material they want. As a parent, and a community member, I think people should be able to protect their homes from imagery - much of it violent - that is, I feel, a form of child abuse when adult society inflicts it upon children.

Naomi Wolf

I want to tell my jokes. I want to have time with my children. I want to entertain people. And at one point, I'll walk away from show business. But I don't want to walk away empty-handed.

Dave Chappelle

Through books and photographs, I saw a world that was not my own - and I realized that there was another world. That's why I'm concerned about education, because it helps our children see other worlds.

Bette Midler

The children who are 'our future' will inherit a world

created not just by parental devotion but by the sort of zealous, focused endeavors that can preclude good parenting.

Virginia Postrel

There's a variety and depth to the song topics I get to write about in children's music and books: being able to write about things I wouldn't normally write about, like a disappointing pancake, or monsters or opposite day is really different than writing about heartbreak and relationships.

Lisa Loeb

'Hell is for Children' is amazing to do every night and 'Promises in the Dark' and 'Love Is a Battlefied,' of course, but my absolute favorite would be 'Heartbreaker.' It's the one that started everything, so it has a very special place in my heart. And it still rocks every night! It's so fun to do.

Pat Benatar

The forefathers of the United States were children of religious bigotry and persecution, and, as a result, fled Britain to create a new approach to life and government. They valued intellect and education. In fact, they outlined the principles of the United States' democracy to establish intellectual freedom from the Church.

Mike Medavoy

We burned to death 100,000 Japanese civilians in Tokyo - men, women and children. LeMay recognized that what he was doing would be thought immoral if his side had lost. But what makes it immoral if you lose and not immoral if you win?

Robert McNamara

Welsh is my mother tongue, and my children speak it. If you come and live in this community you'll work out pretty quickly that it's beneficial to learn the language, because if you're going to the pub or a cafe you need to be a part of the local life.

Bryn Terfel

I wanted to write a book that talked about the emotions of children, which is the rainbow. We all have moods. We talk about being blue when we're sad, and being yellow when we're cowards, and when we're mad, we're red.

Dolly Parton

The siblings of special needs children are quite special. Absolutely accepting and totally loving, from birth, someone who is different mentally, and has a different way of seeing the world, is a wonderful trait. It's a trait I wish there was another way of getting, but there isn't. And it does involve a degree of not having it fantastically easy.

Sally Phillips

Whenever an earthquake or tsunami takes thousands of innocent lives, a shocked world talks of little else. I'll never forget the wrenching days I spent in Haiti last year for Save the Children just weeks after the earthquake.

Anne M. Mulcahy

There are fathers who do not love their children; there is no grandfather who does not adore his grandson.

Victor Hugo

In our ecclesiastical region there are priests who don't baptize the children of single mothers because they weren't conceived in the sanctity of marriage. These are today's hypocrites. Those who clericalize the church. Those who separate the people of God from salvation.

Pope Francis

Healthy children will not fear life if their elders have integrity enough not to fear death.

Erik Erikson

Hugs can do great amounts of good - especially for children.

Princess Diana

Even before I knew I was gay, I knew I didn't want to have a child. I knew I didn't want to have one. I never want to have to release it from me. Listen, I love babies. I love children. And I melt when I'm around them. I also love my freedom and I love that I can sleep at night.

Ellen DeGeneres

Animals are sentient, intelligent, perceptive, funny and entertaining. We owe them a duty of care as we do to children.

Michael Morpurgo

Being considerate of others will take your children further

in life than any college degree.

Marian Wright Edelman

We should not teach children the sciences; but give them a taste for them.

Jean-Jacques Rousseau

Let them look to the past, but let them also look to the future; let them look to the land of their ancestors, but let them look also to the land of their children.

Wilfrid Laurier

Children are remarkable for their intelligence and ardor, for their curiosity, their intolerance of shams, the clarity and ruthlessness of their vision.

Aldous Huxley

I love to go down to the schoolyard and watch all the little children jump up and down and run around yelling and screaming. They don't know I'm only using blanks.

Emo Philips

The training of children is a profession, where we must know how to waste time in order to save it.

Jean-Jacques Rousseau

Women now have choices. They can be married, not married, have a job, not have a job, be married with children, unmarried with children. Men have the same choice we've always had: work, or prison.

Tim Allen

Hunger and malnutrition have devastating consequences for children and have been linked to low birth weight and birth defects, obesity, mental and physical health problems, and poorer educational outcomes.

Marian Wright Edelman

My generation's parents told their children, 'Become an accountant, a lawyer, or an engineer; that will give you a solid foothold in the middle class.' But these jobs are now being sent overseas. So in order to make it today, you have to do work that's hard to outsource, hard to automate.

Daniel H. Pink

I've told my children that when I die, to release balloons in the sky to celebrate that I graduated. For me, death is a graduation.

Elisabeth Kubler-Ross

Be nice to your children. After all, they are going to choose your nursing home.

Steven Wright

Children love their mothers. Especially with a boy child and his mother, there's a bond that's unbreakable.

Tyler Perry

After having children, life becomes about living beyond yourself; about being bigger and better.

Jaclyn Smith

There's plenty to read about keeping your sanity while raising children, but it's all common-sense stuff about task division and taking breaks and the relentlessly repeated magic of date night with your spouse. What's missing is some 'tude.

Jeffrey Kluger

Crowded classrooms and half-day sessions are a tragic waste of our greatest national resource - the minds of our children.

Walt Disney

If children understand that beliefs should be substantiated with evidence, as opposed to tradition, authority, revelation or faith, they will automatically work out for themselves that they are atheists.

Richard Dawkins

First and foremost comes my family and my life with Brad. We have so much joy in raising our children and teaching them about the world that nothing really compares to that.

Angelina Jolie

The gain is not the having of children; it is the discovery of love and how to be loving.

Polly Berrien Berends

Sometimes we know the best thing to do, but fail to do it. New year's resolutions are often like that. We make resolutions because we know it would be better for us to lose weight, or get fit, or spend more time with our children. The problem is that a resolution is generally easier to break than it is to keep.

Peter Singer

The Bible is one of the greatest blessings bestowed by God on the children of men. It has God for its author; salvation for its end, and truth without any mixture for its matter. It is all pure.

John Locke

There's nothing better than having a baby. I've always loved children. I used to work summers at the YMCA and be in charge of, like, 30 preschool kids. I knew that when I had a child, I'd be overwhelmed, and it's true... I can't tell you how much my attitude has changed since we've got Frances. Holding my baby is the best drug in the world.

Kurt Cobain

Child labor and poverty are inevitably bound together and

if you continue to use the labor of children as the treatment for the social disease of poverty, you will have both poverty and child labor to the end of time.

Grace Abbott

In many parts of the world, especially Pakistan and Afghanistan, terrorism, war and conflict stop children to go to their schools. We are really tired of these wars. Women and children are suffering.

Malala Yousafzai

For children, diversity needs to be real and not merely relegated to learning the names of the usual suspects during Black History Month or enjoying south-of-the-border cuisine on Cinco de Mayo. It means talking to and spending time with kids not like them so that they may discover those kids are in fact just like them.

John Ridley

I was quiet, a loner. I was one of those children where, if you put me in a room and gave me some crayons and a pencils, you wouldn't hear from me for nine straight hours. And I was always drawing racing cars and rockets and spaceships and planes, things that were very fast that would take me away.

Gary Oldman

Creativity is the key to success in the future, and primary education is where teachers can bring creativity in children at that level.

A. P. J. Abdul Kalam

Or heritage and ideals, our code and standards - the things we live by and teach our children - are preserved or diminished by how freely we exchange ideas and feelings.

Walt Disney

Play is often talked about as if it were a relief from serious learning. But for children play is serious learning. Play is really the work of childhood.

Fred Rogers

There are only two lasting bequests we can hope to give our children. One of these is roots, the other, wings.

Johann Wolfgang von Goethe

I was a queen, and you took away my crown; a wife, and you killed my husband; a mother, and you deprived me of my children. My blood alone remains: take it, but do not make me suffer long.

Marie Antoinette

I think what you're seeing is a profound recognition on the part of the American people that gays and lesbians and transgender persons are our brothers, our sisters, our children, our cousins, our friends, our co-workers, and that they've got to be treated like every other American. And I think that principle will win out.

Barack Obama

With patient and firm determination, I am going to press on for jobs. I'm going to press on for equality. I'm going to press on for the sake of our children. I'm going to press on for the sake of all those families who are struggling right now. I don't have time to feel sorry for myself. I don't have time to complain. I am going to press on.

Barack Obama

Adults are obsolete children.

Dr. Seuss

We are the children of a technological age. We have found streamlined ways of doing much of our routine work. Printing is no longer the only way of reproducing books. Reading them, however, has not changed.

Lawrence Clark Powell

Just as we teach our children how to ride a bike, we need to teach them how to navigate social media and make the right moves that will help them. The physical world is similar to the virtual world in many cases. It's about being aware. We can prevent many debacles if we're educated.

Amy Jo Martin

One of the very best reasons for having children is to be reminded of the incomparable joys of a snow day.

Susan Orlean

I don't have time for their judgement and their stupidity and you know they lay down with their ugly wives in front of their ugly children and look at their loser lives and then they look at me and they say, 'I can't process it' well, no, you never will stop trying, just sit back and enjoy the show. You know?

Charlie Sheen

I want to rip out his heart and feed it to Lennox Lewis. I want to kill people. I want to rip their stomachs out and eat their children.

Mike Tyson

Cherish your visions and your dreams as they are the children of your soul, the blueprints of your ultimate achievements.

Napoleon Hill

A lot of us grow up and we grow out of the literal interpretation that we get when we're children, but we bear the scars all our life. Whether they're scars of beauty or scars of ugliness, it's pretty much in the eye of the beholder.

Stephen King

When was the last time you spent a quiet moment just doing nothing - just sitting and looking at the sea, or watching the wind blowing the tree limbs, or waves rippling on a pond, a flickering candle or children playing in the park?

Ralph Marston

The relationship between parents and children, but especially between mothers and daughters, is tremendously powerful, scarcely to be comprehended in any rational way.

Joyce Carol Oates

Women are nothing but machines for producing children.

Napoleon Bonaparte

Having children is my greatest achievement. It was my saviour. It switched my focus from the outside to the inside. My children are gifts, they remind me of what's important.

Elle Macpherson

Diabetes is an all-too-personal time bomb which can go off today, tomorrow, next year, or 10 years from now - a time bomb affecting millions like me and the children here today.

Mary Tyler Moore

I appeal to you, my friends, as mothers: are you willing to enslave your children? You stare back with horror and indignation at such questions. But why, if slavery is not wrong to those upon whom it is imposed?

Angelina Grimke

Some people are cool with the fact that their bodies bear witness to this great thing they produced, their children, and I understand that. But on a personal level, it makes me feel better that my breasts are not down to my knees when I'm undressed in front of my husband.

Patricia Heaton

A mother becomes a true grandmother the day she stops noticing the terrible things her children do because she is so enchanted with the wonderful things her grandchildren do.

Lois Wyse

A revolution can be neither made nor stopped. The only thing that can be done is for one of several of its children to give it a direction by dint of victories.

Napoleon Bonaparte

Whenever I date a guy, I think, 'Is this the man I want my children to spend their weekends with?'

Rita Rudner

Being a good mother does not call for the same qualities as being a good housewife; a dedication to keeping children clean and tidy may override an interest in their separate development as individuals.

Ann Oakley

The Hispanic community understands the American Dream and have not forgotten what they were promised - that in the U.S., a free market system, allows us all to succeed economically, achieve stability and security for your family and leave your children better off than yourselves.

Marco Rubio

Too many children in foster care are falling through cracks. Be a hero, take the time learn about adoption today.

Bruce Willis

Parents have no greater responsibility in this world than the bringing up of their children in the right way, and they will have no greater satisfaction as the years pass than to see those children grow in integrity and honesty and make something of their lives.

Gordon B. Hinckley

Why should I marry? One marries to have children, but I already have children! My nieces and nephews are my children.

Salman Khan

I know children regress after vaccination because it happened to my own son. Why aren't there any tests out there on the safety of how vaccines are administered in the real world, six at a time? Why have only two of the 36 shots our kids receive been looked at for their relationship to autism?

Jenny McCarthy

My only purpose is to teach children to rebel against authority figures.

Sherman Alexie

I wanted to write something in a voice that was unique to who I was. And I wanted something that was accessible to the person who works at Dunkin Donuts or who drives a bus, someone who comes home with their feet hurting like my father, someone who's busy and has too many children, like my mother.

Sandra Cisneros

Our censorship has sort of gotten a little too far. Too much censorship is just as bad as having none at all. Children need to be exposed to things, because if they don't see it, eventually, it's not like it's not going to happen, but it's just that there needs to be a balance.

Zoe Saldana

I'm the son of a pediatrician, and I do believe that the most important resource we have is our kids. And I think the most important thing for America's future is to invest more in our children.

Ezekiel Emanuel

The truth is that contraception saves lives, prevents unplanned pregnancies, improves outcomes for children and reduces the number of abortions.

Ann McLane Kuster

South Koreans who have seen and praised the mass games should remember the hardship of tearful children. Teachers drive them hard with curses and orders to repeat and repeat. When the children return home in the evening, they can hardly walk.

Kim Il-sung

I've yet to be on a campus where most women weren't worrying about some aspect of combining marriage, children, and a career. I've yet to find one where many men were worrying about the same thing.

Gloria Steinem

A house without books is like a room without windows. No man has a right to bring up his children without surrounding them with books, if he has the means to buy them.

Horace Mann

Having children is like having a bowling alley installed in your brain.

Martin Mull

I've helped many, many, many children, thousands of children, cancer kids, leukemia kids.

Michael Jackson

Now, I think that I should have known that he was magic all along. I did know it - but I should have guessed that it would be too much to ask to grow old with and see our children grow up together. So now, he is a legend when he would have preferred to be a man.

Jackie Kennedy

Children are the keys of paradise.

Eric Hoffer

So long as little children are allowed to suffer, there is no true love in this world.

Isadora Duncan

Cyberspace. A consensual hallucination experienced daily

by billions of legitimate operators, in every nation, by children being taught mathematical concepts.

William Gibson

The sad truth is that the civil rights movement cannot be reborn until we identify the causes of black suffering, some of them self-inflicted. Why can't black leaders organize rallies around responsible sexuality, birth within marriage, parents reading to their children and students staying in school and doing homework?

Henry Louis Gates

When you see in places like Africa and parts of Asia abject poverty, hungry children and malnutrition around you, and you look at yourself as being people who have well being and comforts, I think it takes a very insensitive, tough person not to feel they need to do something.

Ratan Tata

We say that a girl with her doll anticipates the mother. It is more true, perhaps, that most mothers are still but children with playthings.

F. H. Bradley

Society needs both parents and nonparents, both the work party and the home party. While raising children is the most important work most people will do, not everyone is cut out for parenthood. And, as many a childless teacher has proved, raising kids is not the only important contribution a person can make to their future.

Virginia Postrel

Such is the life of a man. Moments of joy, obliterated by unforgettable sadness. There's no need to tell the children that.

Marcel Pagnol

I was one of those children forced into fighting at the age of 13, in my country Sierra Leone, a war that claimed the lives of my mother, father and two brothers. I know too well the emotional, psychological and physical burden that comes with being exposed to violence as a child or at any age for that matter.

Ishmael Beah

Catholic schools in our Nation's education have been paramount in teaching the values that we as parents seek to instill in our children.

Joe Baca

When you're writing a book, with people in it as opposed to animals, it is no good having people who are ordinary, because they are not going to interest your readers at all. Every writer in the world has to use the characters that have something interesting about them, and this is even more true in children's books.

Roald Dahl

If we are to teach real peace in this world, and if we are to carry on a real war against war, we shall have to begin with the children.

Mahatma Gandhi

Every book is a children's book if the kid can read!

Mitch Hedberg

Welcome to Lake Wobegon, where all the women are strong, all the men are good-looking, and all the children are above average.

Garrison Keillor

Our revenge will be the laughter of our children.

Bobby Sands

Setting a good example for your children takes all the fun out of middle age.

William Feather

Everyone who knows me will know the truth, which is that my children come first in my life and that I would never harm any child.

Michael Jackson

Our children are counting on us to provide two things: consistency and structure. Children need parents who say what they mean, mean what they say, and do what they say they are going to do.

Barbara Coloroso

Today, the news is scandals; that is news, but the many

children who don't have food - that's not news. This is grave. We can't rest easy while things are this way.

Pope Francis

The more people have studied different methods of bringing up children the more they have come to the conclusion that what good mothers and fathers instinctively feel like doing for their babies is the best after all.

Benjamin Spock

If you're an adult and you choose not to believe in science, fine, but please don't prevent your children from learning about it and letting them draw their own conclusions.

Bill Nye

The Internet is just bringing all kinds of information into the home. There's just a lot of distraction, a lot of competition for the parent's voice to resonate in the children's ears.

Phil McGraw

Femininity is part of the God-given divinity within each of

you. It is your incomparable power and influence to do good. You can, through your supernal gifts, bless the lives of children, women, and men. Be proud of your womanhood. Enhance it. Use it to serve others.

James E. Faust

I hate homework. I hate it more now than I did when I was the one lugging textbooks and binders back and forth from school. The hour my children are seated at the kitchen table, their books spread out before them, the crumbs of their after-school snack littering the table, is without a doubt the worst hour of my day.

Ayelet Waldman

My music is best understood by children and animals.

Igor Stravinsky

Through faith in the Lord Jesus alone can we obtain forgiveness of our sins, and be at peace with God; but, believing in Jesus, we become, through this very faith, the children of God; have God as our Father, and may come to Him for all the temporal and spiritual blessings which we need.

George Muller

Of those who die from avoidable, poverty-related causes, nearly 10 million, according to UNICEF, are children under five. They die from diseases such as measles, diarrhea, and malaria that are easy and inexpensive to treat or prevent.

Peter Singer

Coming through the fire and through the storm of life with a strong man, my fiance Ashanti, whom I've been dating for eight months and two wonderful children beside me, I'm just so happy that I have been able to maintain my integrity and get to where I am today with the right energy around me.

Angie Stone

We have to program the mind of the public that age is not ugly. Age is just age. Wake up, American children, and stop listening to other people's voices. Know yourself, be true to yourself and make a contribution. It took me half my life to know myself. I listened to other people's opinions and took them as gospel.

Carmen Dell'Orefice

What could be more lonely than to be enveloped in silence,

to be the last of your people to speak your native tongue, to have no way to pass on the wisdom of the elders, to anticipate the promise of the children. This tragic fate is indeed the plight of someone somewhere roughly every two weeks.

Wade Davis

I am edgy, raw, offensive, vulgar, untruthful, but intelligent. My jokes are always realistic. I do not make fun of children or people who cannot fight back. That is my limitation.

Vir Das

A huge dollar bill is the most accurate way to teach children the real motto of the United States: In the Almighty Dollar We Trust... Until the average American realizes that capitalism damages her livelihood while augmenting the livelihoods of the wealthy, the Almighty Dollar will continue to rule. It certainly is not ruling in our favor.

Kyrsten Sinema

A lot of times, I think that what I do for a living has no integrity. 'Once Upon A Time' has changed that to a certain extent because the reaction we get from children out in the world is so fulfilling, I cannot even articulate it. There's nothing like being greeted as Snow White by a hyperventilating child versus Ginnifer Goodwin.

Ginnifer Goodwin

Fast food chains spend a large amount of marketing to get the attention of children. People form their eating habits as children so they try to nurture clients as youngsters.

Eric Schlosser

As long as you know men are like children, you know everything!

Coco Chanel

Why should society feel responsible only for the education of children, and not for the education of all adults of every age?

Erich Fromm

The solution to adult problems tomorrow depends on large measure upon how our children grow up today.

Margaret Mead

She discovered with great delight that one does not love one's children just because they are one's children but because of the friendship formed while raising them.

Gabriel Garcia Marquez

If children have the ability to ignore all odds and percentages, then maybe we can all learn from them. When you think about it, what other choice is there but to hope? We have two options, medically and emotionally: give up, or Fight Like Hell.

Lance Armstrong

Grown men can learn from very little children for the hearts of little children are pure. Therefore, the Great Spirit may show to them many things which older people miss.

Black Elk

I never met anyone who didn't have a very smart child. What happens to these children, you wonder, when they reach adulthood?

Fran Lebowitz

I don't need a holiday or a feast to feel grateful for my children, the sun, the moon, the roof over my head, music, and laughter, but I like to take this time to take the path of thanks less traveled.

Paula Poundstone

I've told Billy if I ever caught him cheating, I wouldn't kill him because I love his children and they need a dad. But I would beat him up. I know where all of his sports injuries are.

Angelina Jolie

Children are our second chance to have a great parent-child relationship.

Laura Schlessinger

If I am elected President of these United States, I will work with all my energy and soul to restore that America, to lift our eyes to a better future. That future is our destiny. That future is out there. It is waiting for us. Our children deserve it, our nation depends upon it, the peace and freedom of the world require it.

Mitt Romney

Children should have enough freedom to be themselves - once they've learned the rules.

Anna Quindlen

Obviously, you would give your life for your children, or give them the last biscuit on the plate. But to me, the trick in life is to take that sense of generosity between kin, make it apply to the extended family and to your neighbour, your village and beyond.

Tom Stoppard

For me, I don't like it when there is too much interference in our lives. We're not children. It is our own life in our hands.

Eric Cantona

Parents forgive their children least readily for the faults they themselves instilled in them.

Marie von Ebner-Eschenbach

Both young children and old people have a lot of time on their hands. That's probably why they get along so well.

Jonathan Carroll

I am scared easily, here is a list of my adrenaline - production: 1: small children, 2: policemen, 3: high places, 4: that my next movie will not be as good as the last one.

Alfred Hitchcock

Write in such a way as that you can be readily understood by both the young and the old, by men as well as women, even by children.

Ho Chi Minh

The important things are children, honesty, integrity and faith.

Andy Williams

I had real plans for my next decade and felt I'd worked hard enough to earn it. Will I really not live to see my children married? To watch the World Trade Center rise again? To read - if not indeed write - the obituaries of elderly villains like Henry Kissinger and Joseph Ratzinger?

Christopher Hitchens

In every life, there have to be some shadows. Look at me. My life has been filled with sunshine. A beautiful and caring wife. Five healthy children. I got to do what I loved. How many people are that lucky?

Joe Paterno

I merged those two words, black and feminist, because I was surrounded by black women who were very tough and and who always assumed they had to work and rear children and manage homes.

Toni Morrison

If we had paid no more attention to our plants than we have to our children, we would now be living in a jungle of weed.

Luther Burbank

For only by nurturing the minds and strengthening the values of our children can we give them an opportunity to be full, productive citizens, to reach their God-given potential, and to have good jobs right here in Oklahoma.

Brad Henry

If those who wrote and ratified the 14th Amendment had imagined laws restricting immigration - and had anticipated huge waves of illegal immigration - is it reasonable to presume they would have wanted to provide the reward of citizenship to the children of the violators of those laws? Surely not.

George Will

In an era of parental paranoia, lawsuit mania and testing frenzy, we are failing to inspire our children's curiosity, creativity, and imagination. We are denying them opportunities to tinker, discover, and explore - in short, to play.

Darell Hammond

I wish to thank my parents for making it all possible... and I wish to thank my children for making it necessary.

Victor Borge

The essence of parenthood is to make children think that they are the most handsome, intelligent, brilliant person in the world.

Maurice Saatchi

The public health of five million children should not be left to luck or chance.

Jamie Oliver

Parents should conduct their arguments in quiet, respectful tones, but in a foreign language. You'd be surprised what an inducement that is to the education of children.

Judith Martin

Parents who neglect their children, who don't know where they are, who don't know what they're doing, who don't know who they're hanging out with, you're gonna find yourselves spending some quality time with your kids, in jail, together.

Michael Nutter

It's critical that children spend time before they arrive in school in a warm, attractive and inclusive environment, where they can learn through play, master social skills and prepare for formal schooling.

Michael Gove

While I drew, and wept along with the terrified children I was drawing, I really felt the burden I am bearing. I felt that I have no right to withdraw from the responsibility of being an advocate.

Kathe Kollwitz

Above all, we owe it to the children of the world to stop the conflicts and to create new horizons for them.

F. W. de Klerk

You shall love the Lord your God with all your heart and with all your soul and with all your might. And these words that I command you today shall be on your heart. You shall teach them diligently to your children, and shall talk of them when you sit in your house, and when you walk by the way, and when you lie down, and when you rise.

Moses

Children wish fathers looked but with their eyes; fathers that children with their judgment looked; and either may be wrong.

William Shakespeare

We find delight in the beauty and happiness of children that makes the heart too big for the body.

Ralph Waldo Emerson

Children are the anchors of a mother's life.

Sophocles

When we were children we were grateful to those who filled our stockings at Christmas time. Why are we not grateful to God for filling our stockings with legs?

Gilbert K. Chesterton

No parent is perfect; we all can look back and think of things we could've done to help our children be better prepared for adulthood. And sometimes it's best to admit it to them and encourage them to learn from our mistakes.

Billy Graham

The distinction between children and adults, while probably useful for some purposes, is at bottom a specious one, I feel. There are only individual egos, crazy for love.

Niccolo Machiavelli

My children are the reason I laugh, smile and want to get up every morning.

Gena Lee Nolin

It is an old custom amongst Jewish children, to become war-like on the 'L'ag Beomer.' They arm themselves from head to foot with wooden swords, pop-guns and bows and arrows. They take food with them, and go off to wage war.

Sholom Aleichem

We need your help. I need your help. We need money for research. It may not save my life. It may save my children's life. It may save someone you love. And it's very important.

Jim Valvano

Many people want to send their children to faith schools

because they get good exam results, but they're not foolish enough to believe that it's because of faith that they get good exam results.

Richard Dawkins

We learn our belief systems as very little children, and then we move through life creating experiences to match our beliefs. Look back in your own life and notice how often you have gone through the same experience.

Louise L. Hay

And I say the sacred hoop of my people was one of the many hoops that made one circle, wide as daylight and as starlight, and in the center grew one mighty flowering tree to shelter all the children of one mother and one father.

Black Elk

First and foremost, we need to be the adults we want our children to be. We should watch our own gossiping and anger. We should model the kindness we want to see.

Brene Brown

Recommend to your children virtue; that alone can make them happy, not gold.

Ludwig van Beethoven

I grew up in a big family with a lot of kids around, and I definitely want to have children as well.

Heidi Klum

I love to go to the playground and watch the children jumping up and down. They don't know I'm firing blanks.

Emo Philips

If there is anyone dependent on your income - parents, children, relatives - you need life insurance.

Suze Orman

What's done to children, they will do to society.

Karl A. Menninger

In my view, the Christian religion is the most important and one of the first things in which all children, under a free government ought to be instructed.

Noah Webster

Remember to be gentle with yourself and others. We are all children of chance and none can say why some fields will blossom while others lay brown beneath the August sun.

Kent Nerburn

Permissiveness is the principle of treating children as if they were adults; and the tactic of making sure they never reach that stage.

Thomas Szasz

How is it that little children are so intelligent and men so stupid? It must be education that does it.

Alexandre Dumas

I wanted to be a teacher. I love children, so I wanted to deal with children. Then I wanted to be a veterinarian. But by the age of ten or eleven, when I opened my mouth and said, 'Oh, God, what's this?' I kind of knew teaching and being a veterinarian were gonna have to wait.

Whitney Houston

I've never regretted not having children. My mindset in that regard has been constant. I objected to being born, and I refuse to impose life on someone else.

Robert Smith

Adults find pleasure in deceiving a child. They consider it necessary, but they also enjoy it. The children very quickly figure it out and then practice deception themselves.

Elias Canetti

It has always been the prerogative of children and half-wits to point out that the emperor has no clothes. But the half-wit remains a half-wit, and the emperor remains an emperor.

Neil Gaiman

I don't know if I believe in marriage. I believe in family, love and children.

Penelope Cruz

If you want to fight a war on drugs, sit down at your own kitchen table and talk to your own children.

Barry McCaffrey

Children who reach the age of eighteen with their entire skills set composed on Nintendo and eating Doritos have been neglected. Their parents neglected to give them the character traits necessary to live successfully.

Dave Ramsey

God is waiting eagerly to respond with new strength to each little act of self-control, small disciplines of prayer, feeble searching after him. And his children shall be filled if they will only hunger and thirst after what he offers.

Richard Holloway

I believe in imagination. I did Kramer vs. Kramer before I had children. But the mother I would be was already inside me.

Meryl Streep

Emotional 'literacy' implies an expanded responsibility for schools in helping to socialize children. This daunting task requires two major changes: that teachers go beyond their traditional mission and that people in the community become more involved with schools as both active participants in children's learning and as individual mentors.

Daniel Goleman

We are the children of our landscape; it dictates behavior and even thought in the measure to which we are responsive to it.

Lawrence Durrell

The breakdown of the black community, in order to maintain slavery, began with the breakdown of the black family. Men and women were not legally allowed to get married because you couldn't have that kind of love. It might get in the way of the economics of slavery. Your children could be taken from you and literally sold down the river.

Kerry Washington

I love Jesus Christ. I am a Christian... I cry when I see injustice, children dying of hunger.

Hugo Chavez

For in Jesus Christ there is neither male nor female, bond nor free; even you may be the children of God, if you believe in Jesus.

George Whitefield

We are all different. Yet we are all God's children. We are all united behind this country and the common cause of freedom, justice, fairness, and equality. That is what unites us.

Barbara Boxer

We're helping those children who cannot help themselves and giving a push to those who can. We've done it by working together for a common purpose. I see no reason to stop now.

Jane D. Hull

We get strength and encouragement from watching children.

Hayao Miyazaki

I don't want children cursing. I'm very strict on my nieces and my little brother. They have to listen to clean versions of music. Even my music.

Nicki Minaj

Children are born with their own optimism. They have a clarity and a simplicity that we can only wish for.

Meshell Ndegeocello

Children are very smart, in their own stupid way. A child's brain is like a sponge, and you know how smart sponges are.

Steve Carell

I'm not asking that people accept homosexuality. I'm not asking that they believe like I do that it's inborn. I'm not asking that. All I'm saying is don't let these children suffer without a family because of your bias.

Rosie O'Donnell

I'm considered homophobic and crazy about these things

and old fashioned. But I think that the family - father, mother, children - is fundamental to our civilisation.

Rupert Murdoch

Children, even infants, are capable of sympathy. But only after adolescence are we capable of compassion.

Louise J. Kaplan

Children should learn that reading is pleasure, not just something that teachers make you do in school.

Beverly Cleary

It's kind of the yin and yang that fascinate me. That for all the evil men do, there are also people who work obnoxiously long hours and sacrifice their personal lives because it is a calling - if they don't keep our streets safe, if they aren't there to advocate for and save beaten women and children and murder victims, who will?

Lisa Gardner

In 2009, I traveled to South Sudan with my organization PSI. While there, I visited a local school and met with a group of children who had formed a water club. The group learned about how to treat their drinking water and use proper hygiene practices, such as washing their hands before eating or after going to the bathroom.

Mandy Moore

Children themselves know they are being cheated. Ultimately we owe it to our children. They are in school for 190 days a year. Every moment they spend learning is precious. If a year goes by and they are not being stretched and excited, that blights their life.

Michael Gove

During the periods in my marriage when I chose to stay home with my kids rather than work as an attorney, it caused me no end of anxiety. Despite the fact that I knew I was contributing to our family by caring for our children, I still felt that my worth was less because I wasn't earning.

Ayelet Waldman

We tend to think of divorced or complicated families as a modern invention, and that is not at all true. You only have to read the Greek myths to see broken homes, widows, divorce, stepchildren, children trying to get along with new parents.

Rick Riordan

Charity work is very important to me and gives me an opportunity to give back to my community. I've always been a big supporter of many different charities, have donated millions of dollars to them, and it just feels great to do and be able to help others, especially children.

Richard MacDonald

In the last year my wife has noticed me struggling to get downstairs on a Sunday morning. I've two young children and football has been so good to me over the years I don't want to spoil it.

Graeme Le Saux

Krishna children were taught that in the spiritual world there were no parents, only souls and hence this justified their being kept out of view from others, cloistered in separate buildings and sheltered from the evil material world.

Mary Garden

The people of Liberia know what it means to be deprived

of clean water, but we also know what it means to see our children to begin to smile again with a restoration of hope and faith in the future.

Ellen Johnson Sirleaf

The first and continuing argument for the curtailment of working hours and the raising of the minimum age was that education was necessary in a democracy and working children could not attend school.

Grace Abbott

When you're in your 20s, you're a little more carefree; you're single. You have a very different way of looking at the world and experiencing the world. But later in your 30s, when you have children, a career, career obstacles, mortgages, car payments and relationships, you have to negotiate; that's a very different life.

Melissa De Sousa

I have also seen children successfully surmounting the effects of an evil inheritance. That is due to purity being an inherent attribute of the soul.

Mahatma Gandhi

Only God Himself fully appreciates the influence of a Christian mother in the molding of character in her children.

Billy Graham

Someday I want to have children and give them all the love I never had.

Marilyn Monroe

Youth is a wonderful thing. What a crime to waste it on children.

George Bernard Shaw

If you raise your children to feel that they can accomplish any goal or task they decide upon, you will have succeeded as a parent and you will have given your children the greatest of all blessings.

Brian Tracy

Americans want students to get the best education possible. We want schools to prepare children to become good citizens and members of a prosperous American economy.

Bill Gates

From the solemn gloom of the temple children run out to sit in the dust, God watches them play and forgets the priest.

Rabindranath Tagore

Mothers - especially single mothers - are heroic in their efforts to raise our nation's children, but men must also take responsibility for their children and recognize the impact they have on their families' well-being.

Evan Bayh

You see much more of your children once they leave home.

Lucille Ball

Women have simple tastes. They get pleasure out of the conversation of children in arms and men in love.

H. L. Mencken

It is healthier, in any case, to write for the adults one's children will become than for the children one's 'mature' critics often are.

Alice Walker

The influence of a mother upon the lives of her children cannot be measured. They know and absorb her example and attitudes when it comes to questions of honesty, temperance, kindness, and industry.

Billy Graham

A test of a people is how it behaves toward the old. It is easy to love children. Even tyrants and dictators make a point of being fond of children. But the affection and care for the old, the incurable, the helpless are the true gold mines of a culture.

Abraham Joshua Heschel

While children are struggling to be unique, the world around them is trying all means to make them look like everybody else.

A. P. J. Abdul Kalam

Children astound me with their inquisitive minds. The world is wide and mysterious to them, and as they piece together the puzzle of life, they ask 'Why?' ceaselessly.

John C. Maxwell

Parents are usually more careful to bestow knowledge on their children rather than virtue, the art of speaking well rather than doing well; but their manners should be of the greatest concern.

R. Buckminster Fuller

I hate old people, I hate children. I think any celebrity that adopts a child from a third world country is a fool.

Joan Rivers

It's not only children who grow. Parents do too. As much as we watch to see what our children do with their lives, they are watching us to see what we do with ours. I can't tell my children to reach for the sun. All I can do is reach for it, myself.

Joyce Maynard

What gift has providence bestowed on man that is so dear to him as his children?

Marcus Tullius Cicero

However painful the process of leaving home, for parents and for children, the really frightening thing for both would be the prospect of the child never leaving home.

Robert Neely Bellah

Certainly, people can get along without siblings. Single children do, and there are people who have irreparably estranged relationships with their siblings who live full and satisfying lives, but to have siblings and not make the most of that resource is squandering one of the greatest interpersonal resources you'll ever have.

Jeffrey Kluger

Never have children, only grandchildren.

Gore Vidal

My wish for the new millennium is for all children... to grow up wiser, and stronger and more prosperous for the future than ever before.

Hillary Clinton

We don't have enough support for maternal leave and the kinds of things that some of the European countries do. So we still make it hard on women to go into the work force and feel that they can be good at work but then doing the most important job, which is raising your children in a responsible and positive way.

Hillary Clinton

I am tortured when I am away from my family, from my children. I am horribly guilt-ridden.

Jessica Lange

Just think of the tragedy of teaching children not to doubt.

Clarence Darrow

Children do not give up their innate imagination, curiosity, dreaminess easily. You have to love them to get them to do that.

R. D. Laing

We can't understand when we're pregnant, or when our siblings are expecting, how profound it is to have a shared history with a younger generation: blood, genes, humor. It means we were actually here, on Earth, for a time - like the Egyptians with their pyramids, only with children.

Anne Lamott

Please stop teaching my children that everyone gets a trophy just for participating. What is this, the Nobel Prize? Not everybody gets a trophy.

Glenn Beck

Isn't it true that the fault of birth rests somewhat on the child? I believe it's we who led our parents on to bear us, and it's our unborn children who make our flesh itch.

T. E. Lawrence

Children are apt to live up to what you believe of them.

Lady Bird Johnson

I see that children fill the existential hollowness many

people feel; that when we have children, we know they will need us, and maybe love us, but we don't have a clue how hard it is going to be.

Anne Lamott

God gives me the children's ministry heart and patience. This is what He wants. It's awesome. I don't know where He's gonna take it - but God is building this thing.

Willie Aames

Teach your children how to behave with animals. Adopt a pet. Don't go buy one. Please. That's a sin. Let's get these puppy mills out of business.

Shelley Morrison

Left-wing politicians take away your liberty in the name of children and of fighting poverty, while right-wing politicians do it in the name of family values and fighting drugs. Either way, government gets bigger and you become less free.

Harry Browne

It is only when parental feelings are ineffective or too ambivalent or when the mother's emotions are temporarily engaged elsewhere that children feel lost.

Anna Freud

It is only through raising expectations and striving for excellence that our children can reach their full potential.

Brad Henry

When you have kids you do grow up. I have just started realising it now-it changes the world, having children.

David Beckham

We are a continuum. Just as we reach back to our ancestors for our fundamental values, so we, as guardians of that legacy, must reach ahead to our children and their children. And we do so with a sense of sacredness in that reaching.

Paul Tsongas

What is the use of physicians like myself trying to help parents to bring up children healthy and happy, to have them killed in such numbers for a cause that is ignoble?

Benjamin Spock

Children go where they find sincerity and authenticity.

Eric Cantona

One of the darkest, deepest shames so many of us mothers feel nowadays is our fear that we are Bad Mothers, that we are failing our children and falling far short of our own ideals.

Ayelet Waldman

In my generation, except for a few people who'd gone into banking or nursing or something like that, middle-class women didn't have careers. You were to marry and have children and be a nice mother. You didn't go out and do anything. I found that I got restless.

Julia Child

If you want a free society, teach your children what oppression tastes like. Tell them how many miracles it takes to get from here to there. Above all, encourage them to ask questions. Teach them to think for themselves.

Jonathan Sacks

We owe it to our children to be better stewards of the environment. The alternative? - a world without whales. It's too terrible to imagine.

Pierce Brosnan

Don't live vicariously through your kids or try to shape them into who you wanted to be, like the popular kid or an athlete. Children should be given the opportunity to be themselves.

Joan Cusack

Having children, they're not your property. They need to figure out their own views. I think my daughters have a pretty healthy self-awareness, but I can't speak on their behalf.

Annie Lennox

Life has loveliness to sell, all beautiful and splendid things, blue waves whitened on a cliff, soaring fire that sways and sings, and children's faces looking up, holding wonder like a cup.

Sara Teasdale

Having children is fab. They keep me young and make me get up in the morning.

Jo Brand

In most schools, we measure children on what they know. By and large, they have to memorize the content of whatever test is coming up. Because measuring the results of rote learning is easy, rote prevails. What kids know is just not important in comparison with whether they can think.

Sugata Mitra

To separate children from others of similar age and qualifications solely because of their race generates a feeling of inferiority as to their status in the community that may affect their hearts and minds in a way unlikely ever to be undone.

Earl Warren

Mine is the first generation able to contemplate the possibility that we may live our entire lives without going to war or sending our children to war.

Tony Blair

Wrinkles are hereditary. Parents get them from their children.

Doris Day

I think the shyness one feels in childhood is often overcome with time. There are children who hide behind their parents' legs, but you don't see grown-ups hiding behind people. It just doesn't happen. I mean, not that often. People develop social skills over time.

Susan Cain

God bless all the little children in the world.

Richard Dawson

As the mother teaches her children how to express themselves in their language, so one Gypsy musician teaches the other. They have never shown any need for notation.

Franz Liszt

My children are not royal; they just happen to have the Queen for their aunt.

Princess Margaret

I woke in bits, like all children, piecemeal over the years. I discovered myself and the world, and forgot them, and discovered them again.

Annie Dillard

Our life is all about the choices we make, and when I was looking for a mate for life, I really was looking for someone who was a family man, somebody who would embrace my girls as much as they were going to embrace me. I guess I just wasn't finished having children yet.

Joan Lunden

There are moments of opportunity for families; moments they need to put technology away. These include: no phones or texting during meals. No phones or texting when parents pick up children at school - a child is looking to make eye contact with a parent!

Sherry Turkle

Just about every children's book in my local bookstore has an animal for its hero. But then, only a few feet away in the cookbook section, just about every cookbook includes recipes for cooking animals. Is there a more illuminating illustration of our paradoxical relationship with the nonhuman world?

Jonathan Safran Foer

All children start their school careers with sparkling imaginations, fertile minds, and a willingness to take risks with what they think.

Ken Robinson

Most single moms are very poor, uneducated, can't get a job, and if it weren't for government assistance, their kids would be starving to death and never have health care. And that's the story that we're not seeing, and it's unfortunate that we glorify and glamorize the idea of out of children wedlock.

Mike Huckabee

The youngest children have a great capacity for empathy and altruism. There's a recent study that shows even 14-

month-olds will climb across a bunch of cushions and go across a room to give you a pen if you drop one.

Alison Gopnik

I'm particularly proud of my work with the Starkey Hearing Foundation for whom I raised a million dollars in one day on 'Celebrity Apprentice.' They do great work around the world helping deaf children in developing countries get proper attention and free hearing aids.

Marlee Matlin

Just as God's love to us believers, his children, is unalterably the same, whatever may be the manifestations of that love; and as his peace with us is the same, however much our peace may be disturbed; so it is also with regard to our being in fellowship or partnership with him: it remains unalterably the same so far as God is concerned.

George Muller

It's hard to think of anything that is more socially beneficial than raising children well. It needs to be valued and respected, I believe by everyone in public life regardless of your political party.

Kerry Healey

I have seven children by six different mothers. Maybe success was too good to me.

Eazy-E

When you have children, you realize how easy it is to not see them fully, and perhaps miss all those early years. If you are not careful, you can be too absorbed in work, and they will be only too happy to tell you about it later. Being a parent is one of greatest mindfulness practices of all.

Jon Kabat-Zinn

If we just let our vision of the world go forth, and we embrace it entirely, and we don't try to piece together clever diplomacy but just wage a total war, our children will sing great songs about us years from now.

Richard Perle

Is letting our children watch TV a form of child abuse? If our children grow up knowing everything about Britney Spears and nothing about nature or faith, about anything, is that not a form of child abuse?

Patch Adams

Sure, I'd love to have children some day. But world domination comes first.

Aimee Mullins

It would be better, in a way, if any adults present were completely uneducated. There is nothing children like more than passing on information they have just discovered to people who may not already have it - an elderly grandmother, for instance.

Sugata Mitra

'Feminist comedy,' practically an oxymoron, had a couple of good years after WWII. Chalk it up to the forced female autonomy that occurred during wartime, when Rosie the Riveter went to work in the factories, constructing the Allies' war machines while taking charge of the finances, the home, and the children.

Grace Slick

Why give chemotherapy or even antibiotics to people with end-stage Alzheimer's disease? Keep them pain free and clean, love them but don't automatically try to get the last technology-produced breath from them. Start a preschool program instead or do something about the atrocious state of obesity in our children.

Richard Lamm

By his disobedience of God's law, before man had exercised his power to bring children into the earth, not only Adam lost everything for himself, but his children were born as sinners, imperfect, and without the right to live.

Joseph Franklin Rutherford

In elementary school, we should teach nonviolent conflict resolution and healthy communication skills, which will help children cope with issues like rejection and sexuality later in life.

Jane Velez-Mitchell

It's fantastic to strive towards a nice life where you eat nice organic food and your children go to a nice school and you can afford nice clothes and nice perfume and the hypoallergenic make-up. But there's never a day goes by, and I mean this from the bottom of my heart, that I don't think about where I'm from.

Samantha Morton

People don't understand the devastation the murder of a child does to someone. Eighty percent of parents of murdered children wind up in divorce. The only thing you have in common is that horrible sadness. You can't see the joy of your previous life.

John Walsh

We are prophetic interrogators. Why are so many people hungry? Why are so many people and families in our shelters? Why do we have one of six of our children poor, and one of three of these are children of color? 'Why?' is the prophetic question.

Jim Wallis

If you and I desire the blessings of life, of health, of vigor of body and mind; if we desire the destroying angel to pass us by, as he did in the days of the children of Israel, we must obey the Word of Wisdom; then God is bound, and the blessing shall come to us.

Heber J. Grant

I always hired widows with children, because they had to work and didn't have any foolishness about them.

Colonel Sanders

My discrepancy with children in the industry is that they are made famous before they know who they are as human beings.

Corey Feldman

But I was sure of one thing. If God were a father, with children, that cleanliness I had been feeling wasn't God.

Frances Farmer

I have a dream to provide every Chinese, especially children, sufficient milk each day.

Wen Jiabao

Do I believe in coupling? Do I believe in commitment? Do I believe in co-parenting, raising children together, having a family, and growing old with someone? I absolutely believe in all of those things. I just don't believe that you need to be married to do that. I love going to weddings, though. I do love a good wedding.

Laura Wasser

The steel workers have now buried their dead, while the widows weep and watch their orphaned children become objects of public charity. The murder of these unarmed men has never been publicly rebuked by any authoritative officer of the state or federal government.

John L. Lewis

On bad days, I think I'd like to be a plastic surgeon who goes to Third World countries and operates on children in villages with airlifts, and then I think, 'Yeah, right, I'm going to go back to undergraduate school and take all the biology I missed and then go to medical school.' No. No.

Tama Janowitz

When I took office, Liberia began to recover from years of neglect. Our people have brought clean water into the heart of Monrovia to children who have never known water from a tap. Efforts are underway to expand water projects as much as possible throughout the country.

Ellen Johnson Sirleaf

Well, in order to become a grown man, in order to become significant in my family and significant in my children's life, I had to learn my lessons.

Bobby Brown

Why do children dread mathematics? Because of the wrong approach. Because it is looked at as a subject.

Shakuntala Devi

Words are the children of reason and, therefore, can't explain it. They really can't translate feeling because they're not part of it. That's why it bugs me when people try to analyze jazz as an intellectual theorem. It's not. It's feeling.

Bill Evans

If children know there is someone standing over them who knows all the answers, they are less inclined to find the answers for themselves.

Sugata Mitra

There are those who believe that the value of a children's book can be measured only in terms of the moral lessons it tries to impose or the perfect role models it offers. Personally, I happen to think that a book is of extraordinary value if it gives the reader nothing more than a smile or two. In fact, I happen to think that's huge.

Barbara Park

Our parents and grandparents understood this truth deeply. They believed - as we do - that to create jobs, a modern economy requires modern investments: educating, innovating and rebuilding for our children's future. Building an economy to last, from the middle class up, not from the billionaires down.

Martin O'Malley

One of the things I teach my children is that I have always invested in myself, and I have never stopped learning, never stopped growing.

Chesley Sullenberger

Human beings are the only creatures on earth that allow their children to come back home.

Bill Cosby

My childhood should have taught me lessons for my own

fatherhood, but it didn't because parenting can only be learned by people who have no children.

Bill Cosby

Insanity is hereditary; you get it from your children.

Sam Levenson

Every man needs slaves like he needs clean air. To rule is to breathe, is it not? And even the most disenfranchised get to breathe. The lowest on the social scale have their spouses or their children.

Albert Camus

We ought to esteem it of the greatest importance that the fictions which children first hear should be adapted in the most perfect manner to the promotion of virtue.

Plato

Only mothers can think of the future - because they give birth to it in their children.

Maxim Gorky

Let us sacrifice our today so that our children can have a better tomorrow.

A. P. J. Abdul Kalam

It is with children that we have the best chance of studying the development of logical knowledge, mathematical knowledge, physical knowledge, and so forth.

Jean Piaget

Ages of experience have taught humanity that the commitment of a husband and wife to love and to serve one another promotes the welfare of children and the stability of society.

Jack Kingston

Screaming at children over their grades, especially to the point of the child's tears, is child abuse, pure and simple. It's not funny and it's not good parenting. It is a crushing, scarring, disastrous experience for the child. It isn't the least bit funny.

Ben Stein

Women are, in my view, natural peacemakers. As givers and nurturers of life, through their focus on human relationships and their engagement with the demanding work of raising children and protecting family life, they develop a deep sense of empathy that cuts through to underlying human realities.

Daisaku Ikeda

The American Dream is one of success, home ownership, college education for one's children, and have a secure job to provide these and other goals.

Leonard Boswell

You see a child play, and it is so close to seeing an artist paint, for in play a child says things without uttering a word. You can see how he solves his problems. You can also see what's wrong. Young children, especially, have enormous creativity, and whatever's in them rises to the surface in free play.

Erik Erikson

To me there is no picture so beautiful as smiling, bright-eyed, happy children; no music so sweet as their clear and ringing laughter.

P. T. Barnum

Childhood vaccines are one of the great triumphs of modern medicine. Indeed, parents whose children are vaccinated no longer have to worry about their child's death or disability from whooping cough, polio, diphtheria, hepatitis, or a host of other infections.

Ezekiel Emanuel

My father was a man of great charity towards the poor, and compassion for the sick, and also for servants; so much so, that he never could be persuaded to keep slaves, for he pitied them so much: and a slave belonging to one of his brothers being once in his house, was treated by him with as much tenderness as his own children.

Saint Teresa of Avila

The fight for justice against corruption is never easy. It never has been and never will be. It exacts a toll on our self, our families, our friends, and especially our children. In the end, I believe, as in my case, the price we pay is well worth holding on to our dignity.

Frank Serpico

How true Daddy's words were when he said: all children must look after their own upbringing. Parents can only give good advice or put them on the right paths, but the final forming of a person's character lies in their own hands.

Anne Frank

There can be no keener revelation of a society's soul than the way in which it treats its children.

Nelson Mandela

Don't worry that children never listen to you; worry that they are always watching you.

Robert Fulghum

Raising children uses every bit of your being - your heart, your time, your patience, your foresight, your intuition to protect them, and you have to use all of this while trying to figure out how to discipline them.

Nicole Ari Parker

In India, innocent and poor children are victims of child

labor.

Malala Yousafzai

A mother's arms are made of tenderness and children sleep soundly in them.

Victor Hugo

We must teach our children to resolve their conflicts with words, not weapons.

William J. Clinton

In my country of South Africa, we struggled for years against the evil system of apartheid that divided human beings, children of the same God, by racial classification and then denied many of them fundamental human rights.

Desmond Tutu

Close to a billion people - one-eighth of the world's population - still live in hunger. Each year 2 million children die through malnutrition. This is happening at a time when doctors in Britain are warning of the spread of obesity. We are eating too much while others starve.

Jonathan Sacks

It was once said that the moral test of government is how that government treats those who are in the dawn of life, the children; those who are in the twilight of life, the elderly; and those who are in the shadows of life, the sick, the needy and the handicapped.

Hubert H. Humphrey

The most interesting information comes from children, for they tell all they know and then stop.

Mark Twain

When I see children, I see the face of God. That's why I love them so much. That's what I see.

Michael Jackson

I believe that children are our future. Teach them well and let them lead the way. Show them all the beauty they possess inside.

Whitney Houston

See, people are watching you. Especially your children. They're taking in every single thing you do. They are like video cameras with legs. And they are always in the record mode. They learn more from what you do than from what you say.

Joel Osteen

I think we've taken the meaning of Christmas out. People don't stop and think about Jesus or the birth of Jesus. When they think of Christmas, they think of Santa Claus and - for the children, and they think of giving gifts and out-giving the next person of spending their time looking for the right thing for somebody who has everything.

Billy Graham

Most children threaten at times to run away from home. This is the only thing that keeps some parents going.

Phyllis Diller

Only when Christ comes again will the little white children of Alabama walk hand in hand with little black children.

Billy Graham

The fundamental defect of fathers, in our competitive society, is that they want their children to be a credit to them.

Bertrand Russell

Instead of needing lots of children, we need high-quality children.

Margaret Mead

Because parents have power over children. They feel they have to do what their parents say. But the love of money is the root of all evil. And this is a sweet child. And to see him turn like this, this isn't him. This is not him.

Michael Jackson

Never raise your hand to your children - it leaves your midsection unprotected.

Robert Orben

I consider the fact that thousands of children die each day from starvation and a lack of medicine a crisis for humanity and a problem we must collectively attempt to solve.

Alice Walker

Our bodies are shaped to bear children, and our lives are a working out of the processes of creation. All our ambitions and intelligence are beside that great elemental point.

Saint Augustine

Tranquilizers work only if you follow the advice on the bottle - keep away from children.

Phyllis Diller

At least the Pilgrim Fathers used to shoot Indians: the Pilgrim Children merely punch time clocks.

e. e. cummings

You know, nothing is more important than education, because nowhere are our stakes higher; our future depends on the quality of education of our children today.

Arnold Schwarzenegger

There's really no point in having children if you're not

going to be home enough to father them.

Anthony Edwards

As I get older, all sorts of things become less funny. Once one has children, any cruelty involving children becomes far less amusing than when one was at the mercy of one's friends' and relatives' children.

P. J. O'Rourke

God's arrows of affliction are sharp and painful so He can get our attention. He won't let His beloved children get away with sin because He knows it robs us of blessings, opportunities, and even character refinement.

Charles Stanley

Often and often afterwards, the beloved Aunt would ask me why I had never told anyone how I was being treated. Children tell little more than animals, for what comes to them they accept as eternally established.

Rudyard Kipling

What is the price of experience? Do men buy it for a song?

Or wisdom for a dance in the street? No, it is bought with the price of all the man hath, his house, his wife, his children.

William Blake

I will fight for my children on any level so they can reach their potential as human beings and in their public duties.

Princess Diana

Parents are the last people on earth who ought to have children.

Samuel Butler

Between a man and his wife nothing ought to rule but love. Authority is for children and servants, yet not without sweetness.

William Penn

I believe that we parents must encourage our children to become educated, so they can get into a good college that we cannot afford.

Dave Barry

Nations fight against nations, in marriages people fight against each other, children fight against each other. We are in warfare, in a national warfare, and in warfare with each other and with ourselves.

Charles Stanley

You end up as you deserve. In old age you must put up with the face, the friends, the health, and the children you have earned.

Judith Viorst

It should be noted that children at play are not playing about; their games should be seen as their most serious-minded activity.

Michel de Montaigne

Although modesty is natural to man, it is not natural to children. Modesty only begins with the knowledge of evil.

Jean-Jacques Rousseau

Let's not leave an educational vacuum to be filled by

religious extremists who go to families who have no other option and offer meals, housing and some form of education. If we are going to combat extremism then we must educate those very same children.

Hillary Clinton

Feminism encourages women to leave their husbands, kill their children, practice witchcraft, destroy capitalism and become lesbians.

Pat Robertson

Children need models rather than critics.

Joseph Joubert

My mother was a full-time mother. She didn't have much of her own career, her own life, her own experiences... everything was for her children. I will never be as good a mother as she was. She was just grace incarnate. She was the most generous, loving - she's better than me.

Angelina Jolie

All children alarm their parents, if only because you are

forever expecting to encounter yourself.

Gore Vidal

We can't blame children for occupying themselves with Facebook rather than playing in the mud. Our society doesn't put a priority on connecting with nature. In fact, too often we tell them it's dirty and dangerous.

David Suzuki

Children are the most desirable opponents at scrabble as they are both easy to beat and fun to cheat.

Fran Lebowitz

Our awesome responsibility to ourselves, to our children, and to the future is to create ourselves in the image of goodness, because the future depends on the nobility of our imaginings.

Barbara Grizzuti Harrison

Lawyers, I suppose, were children once.

Charles Lamb

Even when freshly washed and relieved of all obvious confections, children tend to be sticky.

Fran Lebowitz

An infinite God can give all of Himself to each of His children. He does not distribute Himself that each may have a part, but to each one He gives all of Himself as fully as if there were no others.

Aiden Wilson Tozer

Any beast can cry over the misfortunes of its own child. It takes a mensch to weep for others' children.

Sam Levenson

My father never raised his hand to any one of his children, except in self-defense.

Fred Allen

Those children who are beaten will in turn give beatings, those who are intimidated will be intimidating, those who are humiliated will impose humiliation, and those whose souls are murdered will murder.

Alice Miller

If you're financially responsible, your children have a much better chance to grow up financially responsible.

Suze Orman

Parents have become so convinced that educators know what is best for their children that they forget that they themselves are really the experts.

Marian Wright Edelman

Our Father's commitment to us, His children, is unwavering. Indeed He softens the winters of our lives, but He also brightens our summers.

Thomas S. Monson

I believe we should encourage children to sing and play instruments from an early age.

Mick Jagger

Whatever happened to the good ole days, when children worked in factories?

Emo Philips

Perfection is terrible; it cannot have children.

Sylvia Plath

A very painful part of being a parent is having really negative feelings about your children when you love them so much.

Louis C. K.

The bearing, rearing, feeding and educating of children; the running of a house with its thousand details; human relationships with their myriad pulls - women's normal occupations in general run counter to creative life, or contemplative life, or saintly life.

Anne Morrow Lindbergh

Feminism is dated? Yes, for privileged women like my daughter and all of us here today, but not for most of our sisters in the rest of the world who are still forced into premature marriage, prostitution, forced labor - they have children that they don't want or they cannot feed.

Isabel Allende

The women that inspire me are the ones who have careers and children; why would I want to limit myself? I've always wanted to have children, and I would never give up that experience for a career. I want to have it all.

Jennifer Aniston

I am on Facebook, but mainly as a way to spy on my children. I find out more about them from their Facebook pages than from what they tell me.

Salman Rushdie

My children were taught at an early age how money works and that it comes from hard work. They've been on a commission - not an allowance - since they were little. They learned that if they worked around the house, they got paid. If they didn't work, they didn't get paid.

Dave Ramsey

I tried Botox one time and was permanently surprised for a couple of months. It was not a cute look for me. My feeling is, I have three children who should know what emotion I'm feeling at the exact moment I'm feeling it... that is critical.

Julia Roberts

I am deeply aware of the disappointment and hurt that my infidelity has caused to so many people, most of all my wife and children.

Tiger Woods

There are things that you cannot talk to your mother and father about, there are things that you cannot talk to your children about.

Shirley Knight

A grandchild is a miracle, but a renewed relationship with your own children is even a greater one.

T. Berry Brazelton

A majority, perhaps as many as 75 percent, of abortion

clinics are in areas with high minority populations. Abortion apologists will say this is because they want to serve the poor. You don't serve the poor, however, by taking their money to terminate their children.

Alveda King

Here's what I see all across this great city - people working together to make Boston a better place to live and to raise children, to grow and pursue dreams.

Thomas Menino

You have to discipline your children, or they won't respect you, law enforcement or God or anyone else.

Phil Robertson

The dogs did bark, the children screamed, Up flew the windows all; And every soul bawled out, Well done! As loud as he could bawl.

William Cowper

Children also have artistic ability, and there is wisdom in there having it! The more helpless they are, the more instructive are the examples they furnish us; and they must be preserved free of corruption from an early age.

Paul Klee

Sometimes we're so concerned about giving our children what we never had growing up, we neglect to give them what we did have growing up.

James Dobson

Being smarter gives you a tailwind throughout life. People who are more intelligent earn more, live longer, get divorced less, are less likely to get addicted to alcohol and tobacco, and their children live longer.

Steven Pinker

I don't think anybody anywhere can talk about the future of their people or of an organization without talking about education. Whoever controls the education of our children controls our future.

Wilma Mankiller

Quite frankly, teachers are the only profession that teach

our children.

Dan Quayle

It's a great mistake, I think, to put children off with falsehoods and nonsense, when their growing powers of observation and discrimination excite in them a desire to know about things.

Anne Sullivan

Education commences at the mother's knee, and every word spoken within hearsay of little children tends toward the formation of character.

Hosea Ballou

My real fantasy if I was to drop out would be to live in a mobile home and be a hippie and drive around festivals and have millions of children - children with dreadlocks and nose rings - and play the flute.

Rachel Weisz

We owe it to our children to equip them with all the capabilities they'll need to thrive in the limitless world beyond the classrooms.

Naveen Jain

With unemployment still abysmally high, the Obama economy is crushing Hispanics' dreams for their children to live a better life.

Marco Rubio

Most of the people who will walk after me will be children, so make the beat keep time with short steps.

Hans Christian Andersen

The reason most of the children are having problems in any inner-city neighborhood is because they don't see enough positive role models in their own environment.

Marla Gibbs

The world sees in our conduct, in our behaviour, the proof that we are the real children of God.

Pope Shenouda III

We stand our best chance of leaving a legacy to those who want to learn, our children, by standing firm. In matters of style, hey, swing with the stream. But in matters of principle, you need to stand like a rock.

Kevin Costner

Ironically, parenting is a shame and judgment minefield precisely because most of us are wading through uncertainty and self-doubt when it comes to raising our children.

Brene Brown

In my wildest imagination, I never thought that the fifth of six children born to Helen and Buddy Watts - in a poor black neighborhood, in the poor rural community of Eufaula, Oklahoma - would someday be called Congressman.

J. C. Watts

I urge you children to be patient with your parents. If they seem to be out of touch on such vital issues as dating, clothing styles, modern music, and use of family cars, listen to them anyway. They have the experience that you lack.

Joseph B. Wirthlin

I'm not only a lawyer, I have a post doctorate degree in federal tax law from William and Mary. I work in serious scholarship and work in the United States federal tax court. My husband and I raised five kids. We've raised 23 foster children. We've applied ourselves to education reform. We started a charter school for at-risk kids.

Michele Bachmann

Without in any way minimising the economic and psychological blow that people experience when they lose their jobs, the unemployed in affluent countries still have a safety net, in the form of social security payments, and usually free healthcare and free education for their children. They also have sanitation and safe drinking water.

Peter Singer

When fast food is not a treat but a dietary staple, the children surf the internet all day in dark corners of the room and are bombarded with latest gadgets. Things replace parental standards.

Diane Abbott

My wife once said that one of her great ambitions was to

walk down the streets of Hong Kong with her children. So we all went to Asia on one occasion. Then she said she'd like to walk down the streets of Jerusalem with her children. So we arranged our family finances and all went to Jerusalem.

Gordon B. Hinckley

The word tomorrow was invented for indecisive people and for children.

Ivan Turgenev

I'm one of these children who grew up at the knee of my grandmother and her elder sister, listening to very old people talk about their memories.

Hilary Mantel

In times of conflict, war, poverty or religious fundamentalism, women and children are the first and most numerous victims. Women need all their courage today.

Isabel Allende

And I asked my mother about it; I said, 'Is there something

wrong?' She said, 'God... God makes people. You understand that, don't you?' And I said, 'Yeah!' She said, 'Who makes a rainbow?" I said, 'God.' She said, 'I never presumed to tell anyone who could make a rainbow what color to make children.'

Richard Dawson

You cannot write for children They're much too complicated. You can only write books that are of interest to them.

Maurice Sendak

Throughout history no one has suffered more than God. He has suffered because his own children fell away from him. Ever since the Fall, God has been working tirelessly for the restoration of mankind. People do not know this brokenhearted aspect of God.

Sun Myung Moon

At this point in my career, I don't have to deal with audition rejections. So I get my rejection from other things. My children can make me feel rejected. They can humble you pretty quick.

Al Pacino

You can take things that Jimi Hendrix took, from Curtis Mayfield or from Buddy Guy for example, because we are all children of everything, even Picasso. But if you want to stand out, you have to learn to crystallize your existence and create your own fingerprints.

Carlos Santana

If I get the forty additional years statisticians say are likely coming to me, I could fit in at least one, maybe two new lifetimes. Sad that only one of those lifetimes can include being the mother of young children.

Anna Quindlen

My comedy is for children from three to 93. You do need a slightly childish sense of humour and if you haven't got that, it's very sad.

Norman Wisdom

We are spirit children of a loving Heavenly Father who placed us in mortality to see if we would choose - freely choose - to keep His commandments and come unto His Beloved Son. They do not compel us. They cannot, for that would interfere with the plan of happiness. And so there is in us a God-given desire to be responsible for our own choices.

Henry B. Eyring

What do we tell our children? Haste makes waste. Look before you leap. Stop and think. Don't judge a book by its cover. We believe that we are always better off gathering as much information as possible and spending as much time as possible in deliberation.

Malcolm Gladwell

Most adults, unlike most children, understand the difference between a book that will hold them spellbound for a rainy Sunday afternoon and a book that will put them in touch with a part of themselves they didn't even know existed.

Mark Haddon

I think having children is the most amazing thing.

Rachel Stevens

'The Accursed' is very much a novel about social injustice

as the consequence of the terrible, tragic division of classes - the exploitation not only of poor and immigrant workers but of their young children in factories and mills - and as the consequence of race hatred in the aftermath of the Civil War and the freeing of the slaves.

Joyce Carol Oates

All my children inherited perfect pitch.

Chevy Chase

When The Muppet Show ended, we all sat around and said, what kind of television show would we like to do. We felt the need these days are for some quality children's programming.

Jim Henson

Access to books and the encouragement of the habit of reading: these two things are the first and most necessary steps in education and librarians, teachers and parents all over the country know it. It is our children's right and it is also our best hope and their best hope for the future.

Michael Morpurgo

I have a beautiful wife and two beautiful children, and every day I am paid to do what I love.

Treat Williams

I am glad that I do not have any children.

Anna Freud

Let's remember that our children's spirits are more important than any material things. When we do, self-esteem and love blossoms and grows more beautifully than any bed of flowers ever could.

Jack Canfield

The liberation children experience when they discover the Internet is quickly counteracted by the lure of e-commerce web sites, which are customized to each individual user's psychological profile in order to maximize their effectiveness.

Douglas Rushkoff

Children have a right to some stability and constancy from the adults in their lives.

Dan Savage

Cloning looks like a degrading of parenthood and a perversion of the right relation between parents and children.

Leon Kass

Washington's insatiable desire to spend our children's inheritance on failed stimulus plans and other misguided economic theories have given record debt and left us with far too many unemployed.

Rick Perry

Circulating through the children's ward and seeing terminally ill kids, heads shaved, smiling and having a ball despite the tubes and needles sticking into them, I thought: What do I have to worry about? If God takes me, at least I've lived for 35 years.

Eric Davis

Sociologists well understand that chaos at home causes violent behavior, educational failure and social alienation among children. Yet, many of us in America stay far, far away from this topic. That in itself is a national scandal. Bad parenting is gravely harming this nation.

Bill O'Reilly

Of those who die from avoidable, poverty-related causes, nearly 10 million, according to UNICEF, are children under five. They die from diseases such as measles, diarrhoea, and malaria that are easy and inexpensive to treat or prevent.

Peter Singer

Sometimes when I visit my sister and her two children, I wonder if she missed a lot by getting married. Right now, nothing could be further from my mind than getting married.

Natalie Wood

When I tell children that they are far too dependent on their gizmos, they do not deny it. But they really don't care. This is their real life - texting about trivial things; listening to numbing music on their private headphones. The machines block everything out - you create your own little trivial world.

Bill O'Reilly

I always felt that at the moment I was born, God must have blinked. He missed the occasion and never knew I had arrived. My parents had 11 children. While I love them and my five brothers and five sisters deeply, some days I felt lost in the litter.

Regina Brett

I didn't start sweating until I had children. That was one of the first things I realized when my daughter Violet was born - I started getting wicked BO. You know there's a difference between basketball BO and stress BO? This was definitely stress BO. Like, new dad BO.

Dave Grohl

Everybody has an inferiority complex when they step into a room. But then when you have children and you get older, it doesn't really matter. When I was young I had so many inferiority complexes. I had an inferiority complex because I didn't go to university. I had an inferiority complex because I didn't train.

Helena Bonham Carter

God offers us counsel not just for our own safety, but for

the safety of His other children, whom we should love. There are few comforts so sweet as to know that we have been an instrument in the hands of God in leading someone else to safety. That blessing generally requires the faith to follow counsel when it is hard to do.

Henry B. Eyring

I love developing children as characters. Children rarely have important roles in literary fiction - they are usually defined as cute or precious, or they create a plot by being kidnapped or dying.

Barbara Kingsolver

I have been married twice, and those were not the happiest times of my life. Part of the problem, quite frankly, is that when you get married, the romance disappears and the children arrive and the love is transferred. It shouldn't be that way, but too often it is transferred to the children.

Hugh Hefner

Let your children be as so many flowers, borrowed from God. If the flowers die or wither, thank God for a summer loan of them.

Samuel Rutherford

When tragedy strikes, or even when it looms, our families will have the opportunity to look into our hearts to see whether we know what we said we knew. Our children will watch, feel the Spirit confirm that we lived as we preached, remember that confirmation, and pass the story across the generations.

Henry B. Eyring

Many will view the compromises that will be made during your negotiations as painful concessions. But why not view them as peace offerings, ones that will provide in return the priceless gifts of hope, security and freedom for our children and our children's?

Abdallah II of Jordan

Another hero was Tom Swift, in the books. What he stood for, the freedom, the scientific knowledge and being and engineer gave him the ability to invent solutions to problems. He's always been a hero to me. I buy old Tom Swift books now and read them to my own children.

Steve Wozniak

Our nation's oldest sin and deepest crime is the isolation of minority children - black children, in particular - in schools that are not only segregated but shamefully unequal.

Jonathan Kozol

Hate and mistrust are the children of blindness.

William Watson

Is Valentine's Day a day to make cupcakes with your children? No, Valentine's is supposed to be a day about romantic love.

Ayelet Waldman

The value of marriage is not that adults produce children but that children produce adults.

Peter De Vries

From an evolutionary perspective children are, literally, designed to learn. Childhood is a special period of protected immaturity. It gives the young breathing time to master the things they will need to know in order to survive as adults.

Alison Gopnik

True revolutionaries are like God - they create the world in their own image. Our awesome responsibility to ourselves, to our children, and to the future is to create ourselves in the image of goodness, because the future depends on the nobility of our imaginings.

Barbara Grizzuti Harrison

It's fairness to say those who work hard, get up in the morning, cut their cloth - in other words 'we can only afford to have one or two children because we don't earn enough'. They pay their taxes and they want to know that the same kind of decision-making is taking place for those on benefits.

Iain Duncan Smith

What our children have to fear is not the cars on the highways of tomorrow but our own pleasure in calculating the most elegant parameters of their deaths.

J. G. Ballard

Do the elected officials in Washington stand with ordinary Americans - working families, children, the elderly, the poor - or will the extraordinary power of billionaire campaign contributors and Big Money prevail? The American people, by the millions, must send Congress the answer to that question.

Bernie Sanders

I've been sober for two-and-a-half years, My children are happy. In August, my wife and I will celebrate our fifteenth wedding anniversary. My band is back together with a sold-out tour.

Trey Anastasio

We apologise for the laws and policies of successive parliaments and governments that have inflicted profound grief, suffering and loss on these our fellow Australians. We apologise especially for the removal of Aboriginal and Torres Strait Islander children from their families, their communities and their country.

Kevin Rudd

Increased physical activity during the school day can help children's attention, classroom behavior, and achievement test scores. Meanwhile, the decline of play is closely linked to ADHD; behavioral problems; and stunted social, cognitive, and creative development.

Darell Hammond

One of the reasons it's important for me to write about war is I really think that the concept of war, the specifics of war, the nature of war, the ethical ambiguities of war, are introduced too late to children. I think they can hear them, understand them, know about them, at a much younger age without being scared to death by the stories.

Suzanne Collins

Experts say that if children can't read by the end of the fifth grade, they lose self-confidence and self-esteem, making them more likely to enter the juvenile justice system.

Dirk Kempthorne

Positive social emotions like compassion and empathy are generally good for us, and we want to encourage them. But do we know how to most reliably raise children to care about the suffering of other people? I'm not sure we do.

Sam Harris

Many schools today are sacrificing social studies, the arts and physical education so children can cover basic subjects like math, English and science.

Geoffrey Canada

Even the classics that we read to our young children are full of wolves' fangs and burning ovens and bloody feet and ice shards piercing hearts. Even the New Testament climaxes with an act of unspeakable torture. Might as well just read to our kids from the Amnesty Annual Report and be done with it.

Geraldine Brooks

Although children are only 24 percent of the population, they're 100 percent of our future and we cannot afford to provide any child with a substandard education.

Ed Markey

The only thing that I can do is know that I have great confidence in raising children and being a great mother.

Cheryl Tiegs

I don't like games. You're robbing the precious time of children to be children. They need to be in touch with the real world more.

Hayao Miyazaki

It surprises me how much children like me, you know? If they look at me as an example, I have a big responsibility.

Mario Balotelli

In Chinese culture, it wouldn't occur to kids to question or talk back to their parents. In American culture, kids in books, TV shows and movies constantly score points with their snappy back talk. Typically, it's the parents who need to be taught a life lesson - by their children.

Amy Chua

Roaring like a tiger turns some children into pianists who debut at Carnegie Hall but only crushes others. Coddling gives some the excuse to fail and others the chance to succeed.

Ayelet Waldman

It is the parent's job to see how their child learns and to make sure that the children's self confidence is buoyed at all times, or they will plummet like a stone.

Henry Winkler

Around 1998, I went through lots of pressures and struggles. My children got married within eight months of each other, my son was diagnosed with cancer and went through major surgery and radiation, my mother had five life-threatening hospitalizations where I stayed with her, my husband's dental office burned to the ground.

Anne Graham Lotz

Except I'm aware that as a writer you can't get away with as much writing for children as you can with adults. Children have much more finely tuned senses of justice, morals, and ethics. They are much more Platonic: children are symmetrical, before we begin to fragment them with our own nonsensical ideas and squelch their natural joy in knowledge.

Alan Bradley

It's long been accepted as fact that the availability of family planning services saves lives. Where women have access to these services, children and families are healthier, and society at large benefits.

Martha Plimpton

My experience as a school nurse taught me that we need to make a concerted effort, all of us, to increase physical fitness activity among our children and to encourage all Americans to adopt a healthier diet that includes fruits and vegetables, but there is more.

Lois Capps

So many organizations have a mentoring arm, but they don't really do it. Their idea of mentoring a kid is giving them general advice. But what they need to do is read with children.

Walter Dean Myers

My theory is children don't do what you tell them to do, they do what you do. You have to always do the right thing because they follow you.

Boman Irani

There's nothing like a love for our children. I love being a papa, and that's the truth.

Richie Sambora

No race of barbarians ever existed yet offered up children for money.

Samuel Gompers

Years ago I wanted to buy an apartment in New York City. I was a single female - I had gone through my divorce - I had three children, I was in show business and black. It was, like, impossible.

Diana Ross

It is a matter of public shame that while we have now commemorated our hundredth anniversary, not one in every ten children attending Public schools throughout the colonies is acquainted with a single historical fact about Australia.

Henry Lawson

Restaurants are like having children: it's fun to make them, maybe, but then you have them for good and bad. You are going to have to raise them and if something goes wrong when they are 30 years old, they will still be your little boy.

Wolfgang Puck

Every day we do get closer to a cure. Three out of four children who are diagnosed with cancer will survive the disease, but that is not good enough. The loss of one child to this disease is too much.

Michael McCaul

My father was frightened of his mother; I was frightened of my father, and I am damned well going to see to it that my children are frightened of me.

King George V

When people said Africa would change me, I didn't understand what they meant. To see the poverty in the townships, for instance, is overwhelming. I found it heart-wrenching to see young children walking barefoot and hungry in the dirt. I'm the kind of person who wants to change the world right here and now, so I got frustrated.

Jennifer Hudson

Generosity has built America. When we fail to invest in children, we have to pay the cost.

Bob Keeshan

All these fifty-year-old guys wearing baseball caps and shorts and acting like children. It winds me up. Men don't have to take responsibility anymore. Most of the guys I know would punch me on the nose for saying this, but maybe we do have to bring back conscription.

Chrissie Hynde

Contaminated food is a major cause of diarrhea, substantially contributing to malnutrition and killing about 2.2 million people each year, most of them children.

Gro Harlem Brundtland

I'd rather be dealt with as a person than a persona. With my children, I'm just 'Mom.' At the end of the day, the position is just a position, a title is just a title, and those things come and go. It's really your essence and your values that are important.

Queen Rania of Jordan

Yes, yes, children must early be made to practise piety, godliness, and propriety; a person of good breeding is one into whom 'good maxims' have been instilled and impressed, poured in through a funnel, thrashed in and preached in.

Max Stirner

We need a pedagogy free from fear and focused on the magic of children's innate quest for information and understanding.

Sugata Mitra

Common Core, the initiative that claims to more accurately measure K-12 student knowledge in English and math, also encourages children to step up their 'critical thinking.'

David Harsanyi

When you are happy and in love and when you have children, then maybe you are beautiful.

Emmanuelle Beart

The most important part of the process of mourning is regularly reciting kaddish in a synagogue. Kaddish is a doxology, which Jewish tradition has mandated children to recite daily in a synagogue during the year of mourning for a deceased parent and then on the anniversary of his or her death thereafter.

David Novak

These days, children can text on their cell phone all night long, and no one else is seeing that phone. You don't know who is calling that child.

Kamala Harris

I would love to have a complete family. I'd love to do it all at once. I'd love to be able to give to my children what my parents were able to give to me. And if I'm blessed to be able to do that, fantastic. If I'm not, then life goes on. You have to do the best you can. I do think we have to bring the family back; I do.

Michael Ealy

Give the children an opportunity to make garden. Let them grow what they will. It matters less that they grow good plants than that they try for themselves.

Liberty Hyde Bailey

Many of the books I loved as a kid, that even my mother read as a child, are very slow going. Today's children are not as patient. The best example of this is 'The Secret Garden,' which I adored as a child.

Lois Lowry

When my children were born, I didn't have them baptized because I felt baptism was about erasing Original Sin - something the Church said children got from their mother - and I absolutely refused to believe women carry Original Sin.

Olympia Dukakis

Parents learn a lot from their children about coping with life.

Muriel Spark

I am a professional photographer because it is the best way I know to earn the money I require to take care of my wife and children.

Irving Penn

Unborn children do not have a voice, but they are young members of the human family. It is time to look at the unborn child, and recognize that it is really a young human, who can feel pain and should be treated with care.

Sam Brownback

Most of us remember adolescence as a kind of double negative: no longer allowed to be children, we are not yet capable of being adults.

Julian Barnes

The beauty about living in Atlanta is that there aren't too many paparazzi here; you can just relax. And that really works for me and my children.

Usher

I wouldn't just come home from school and watch TV everyday, they had me involved in lots of local theatre. I was a very dramatic, talkative child. And that was part of my mother's creative solution - to put me in workshops and classes and children's theatre programmes.

Kerry Washington

I nursed men back to sanity who were driven to despair. I solicited clothes for the ragged children, for the desperate mothers. I laid out the dead, the martyrs of the strike.

Mary Harris Jones

A society of 'children first' is a society that nurtures smiling faces in everyone.

Yoshihiko Noda

To me, Slow parenting is about bringing balance into the home. Children need to strive and struggle and stretch themselves, but that does not mean childhood should be a race. Slow parents give their children plenty of time and space to explore the world on their own terms.

Carl Honore

Despite the best of efforts, many foster children are neither reunited with their families, nor adopted.

Charles Bass

Family life is tough, I'll say that for it. But in my case, I've mined the family. In a sense, I've used it. I've used what happened - the different events, the births of children, birthdays. Connecting, not connecting. Regret, shame, guilt. I mean, they're all in the songs. And love, too, I hasten to add.

Loudon Wainwright III

I am sure that the sad days and happenings were rare, and that I lived the joyous and careless life of other children; but just because the happy days were so habitual to me they made no impression upon my mind, and I can no longer recall them.

Pierre Loti

All children are born pure egoists. They perceive their needs to the exclusion of all others. Only through socialization do they learn that some forms of gratification must be deferred and others denied.

Andrew Vachss

Typically diagnosed during childhood and adolescent years, juvenile diabetes, also referred to as Type I diabetes, currently affects more than 3 million Americans and more then 13,000 children are diagnosed each year.

Elijah Cummings

Inspire your children. I promise, your kids will think you're cool if you do this. They may not tell you that now, but they'll thank you later in life.

Laura Marano

For women of a certain age, how do you meet a guy, fall in love, and decide he's the right man to have children with? Your clock's ticking, you're looking at him, and it's a crazy, pressure-filled experience.

Marcia Cross

If you love your children, if you love your country, if you love the God of love, clear your hands from slaves, burden not your children or your country with them.

Richard V. Allen

I want to help others 'think first' before diving into a pool or lake to prevent these types of life-changing accidents. I know I'm in a very fortunate minority and hope my story inspires both adults and children to be more careful.

Brooke Burns

Children need to trust and depend upon those who are
responsible for them.

Gordon Neufeld

The primary school I attended in Shanghai was a very
liberal one, established by scholars who had return from an
education in France. The children of leading families were
enrolled there, including the son of a well-known man
believed to be a top gangster of the underworld!

Charles K. Kao

You bring children into the world. You love them with
heart and soul.

Alice Walker

Children's talent to endure stems from their ignorance of
alternatives.

Maya Angelou

My greatest blessing has been the birth of my son. My next
greatest blessing has been my ability to turn people into

children of mine.

Maya Angelou

Nothing I've ever done has given me more joys and rewards than being a father to my children.

Bill Cosby

You know the only people who are always sure about the proper way to raise children? Those who've never had any.

Bill Cosby

I really wanted to retire and rest and spend more time with my children, my grandchildren and of course with my wife.

Nelson Mandela

People say children are charming because they tell the truth. That's a lie. I've got five of them. They only tell the truth if they're in pain.

Bill Cosby

You are the bows from which your children as living arrows are sent forth.

Khalil Gibran

Raising children is an incredibly hard and risky business in which no cumulative wisdom is gained: each generation repeats the mistakes the previous one made.

Bill Cosby

In America there are two classes of travel - first class, and with children.

Robert Benchley

Poets have said that the reason to have children is to give yourself immortality. Immortality? Now that I have five children, my only hope is that they are all out of the house before I die.

Bill Cosby

Our children are angry. The profanity is out in the street. It's on the buses and in the subway. Our children are trying to tell us something, and we are not listening.

Bill Cosby

What we need is for people to realize - 'I want to raise my kid. I want to go back and get my three kids. I want to take on that responsibility. I want to love my children.'

Bill Cosby

I want to get violence - I want schools to start from K through 12 to just every day have teachers understand that they don't want to talk about anything that is violent, and they want to explain to the children how bad violence is and how behavior - violent behavior, is something that they really should not practice and think about.

Bill Cosby

There are teachers in the United States who cry in the daytime because they see a child or children who haven't eaten properly, children who haven't used soap in so long.

Bill Cosby

Children are all foreigners.

Ralph Waldo Emerson

The thing I want more than anything else? I want to have children. I used to feel for every child I had, I would adopt another.

Marilyn Monroe

Don't handicap your children by making their lives easy.

Robert A. Heinlein

Your children will see what you're all about by what you live rather than what you say.

Wayne Dyer

All men are children, and of one family. The same tale sends them all to bed, and wakes them in the morning.

Henry David Thoreau

According to Ethiopian custom, parents wait to name a baby because children often die in the first weeks of life.

Bill Gates

Living on $6 a day means you have a refrigerator, a TV, a cell phone, your children can go to school. That's not possible on $1 a day.

Bill Gates

I remember thinking quite logically that I didn't want to spoil my children with wealth and so that I would create a foundation, but not knowing exactly what it would focus on.

Bill Gates

When there is no job related stress, you are more aware of your mate and children, if you are a parent.

Zig Ziglar

Somewhere it is written that parents who are critical of other people's children and publicly admit they can do better are asking for it.

Erma Bombeck

As youngsters, my mother taught her children that while we

might not be the smartest people around, we could be courteous, polite and considerate of others.

Zig Ziglar

Mothers play an important role as the heart of the home, but this in no way lessens the equally important role fathers should play, as head of the home, in nurturing, training, and loving their children.

Ezra Taft Benson

I purposely don't talk about money, because people are already skeptical about TV preachers. But I do say that I want you to be blessed. To me, prosperity is having health, having great children, having peace, good relationships. It's not about the money.

Joel Osteen

I try to speak my points of view about black America, and how I feel about black men and the role that black men should play in their lives with their children and in their lives with their women.

Will Smith

We cannot fashion our children after our desires, we must have them and love them as God has given them to us.

Johann Wolfgang von Goethe

If children grew up according to early indications, we should have nothing but geniuses.

Johann Wolfgang von Goethe

It goes without saying that you should never have more children than you have car windows.

Erma Bombeck

Unlike grown ups, children have little need to deceive themselves.

Johann Wolfgang von Goethe

Age merely shows what children we remain.

Johann Wolfgang von Goethe

The run I was on made Sinatra, Flynn, Jagger, Richards, all

of them look like droopy-eyed armless children.

Charlie Sheen

I see children, all children, as humanity's most precious resource, because it will be to them that the care of the planet will always be left.

Alice Walker

Anyone who hates children and animals can't be all bad.

W. C. Fields

A Sunday school is a prison in which children do penance for the evil conscience of their parents.

H. L. Mencken

I think that there's no doubt that as I see friends, families, children of gay couples who are thriving, you know, that has an impact on how I think about these issues.

Barack Obama

I wrote a few children's books... not on purpose.

Steven Wright

I think about my own sons and my own daughters, and I'm sure that many parents are concerned about what their children are exposed to.

Billy Graham

The theory seems to be that as long as a man is a failure he is one of God's children, but that as soon as he succeeds he is taken over by the Devil.

H. L. Mencken

Our acts make or mar us, we are the children of our own deeds.

Victor Hugo

We must do everything in our power to cease the behaviour that makes children everywhere feel afraid.

Alice Walker

You know your children are growing up when they stop asking you where they came from and refuse to tell you where they're going.

P. J. O'Rourke

Many societies have educated their male children on the simple device of teaching them not to be women.

Margaret Mead

Children are unpredictable. You never know what inconsistency they are going to catch you in next.

Henry Ward Beecher

Children are the hands by which we take hold of heaven.

Henry Ward Beecher

Children should neither be seen or heard from - ever again.

W. C. Fields

Occasionally I've seen children become heavy-handed and

insensitive when dealing with their aging parents, and it only caused resentment and hard feelings.

Billy Graham

Children are a wonderful gift. They have an extraordinary capacity to see into the heart of things and to expose sham and humbug for what they are.

Desmond Tutu

Part of our tradition as black women is that we are universalists. Black children, yellow children, red children, brown children, that is the black woman's normal, day-to-day relationship. In my family alone, we are about four different colors.

Alice Walker

Parents, however old they and we may grow to be, serve among other things to shield us from a sense of our doom. As long as they are around, we can avoid the fact of our mortality; we can still be innocent children.

Jane Howard

I have never once regretted missing a business opportunity so that I could be with my children and grandchildren.

Mitt Romney

I have accepted a seat in the House of Representatives, and thereby have consented to my own ruin, to your ruin, and to the ruin of our children. I give you this warning that you may prepare your mind for your fate.

John Adams

A lot of parents today are terrified that something they say to their children might make them 'feel bad.' But, hey, if they've done something wrong, they should feel bad. Kids with a sense of responsibility, not entitlement, who know when to experience gratitude and humility, will be better at navigating the social shoals of college.

Amy Chua

Peace is one of the most precious gifts God has promised His children. I know, because for many years my life was not peaceful, and I was miserable.

Joyce Meyer

Every act of conscious learning requires the willingness to suffer an injury to one's self-esteem. That is why young children, before they are aware of their own self-importance, learn so easily.

Thomas Szasz

There are hundreds of millions of gun owners in this country, and not one of them will have an accident today. The only misuse of guns comes in environments where there are drugs, alcohol, bad parents, and undisciplined children. Period.

Ted Nugent

I think the part of media that romanticizes criminal behavior, things that a person will say against women, profanity, being gangster, having multiple children with multiple men and women and not wanting to is prevalent. When you look at the majority of shows on television they placate that kind of behavior.

Bill Cosby

Instead of being presented with stereotypes by age, sex, color, class, or religion, children must have the opportunity to learn that within each range, some people are loathsome and some are delightful.

Margaret Mead

Give me four years to teach the children and the seed I have sown will never be uprooted.

Vladimir Lenin

Crimes against children are the most heinous crime. That, for me, would be a reason for capital punishment because children are innocent and need the guidance of an adult society.

Clint Eastwood

There is a Providence that protects idiots, drunkards, children and the United States of America.

Otto von Bismarck

When we, through our educational culture, through the media, through the entertainment culture, give our children the impression that human beings cannot control their passions, we are telling them, in effect, that human beings cannot be trusted with freedom.

Alan Keyes

Whenever I want to laugh, I read a wonderful book, 'Children's Letters to God.' You can open it anywhere. One I read recently said, 'Dear God, thank you for the baby brother, but what I prayed for was a puppy.'

Maya Angelou

I'm the one person who wears the words 'hustle, loyalty, respect' on my T-shirts and merchandise. My audience is children. It's very flattering to see a kid wear your T-shirt; it's even more flattering to have a dad come up to you and say, 'I watch you with my kid. Keep doing what you're doing. You're a role model for my son.'

John Cena

Motherhood has taught me the meaning of living in the moment and being at peace. Children don't think about yesterday, and they don't think about tomorrow. They just exist in the moment.

Jessalyn Gilsig

Never have more children than you have car windows.

Erma Bombeck

It is painful to watch children trying to show off for parents who are engrossed in their cell phones. Children are nostalgic for the 'good old days' when parents used to read to them without the cell phone by their side or watch football games or Disney movies without having the BlackBerry handy.

Sherry Turkle

I always have this image of a woman running across a desert carrying children, trying to find water and food, not knowing when they'll get that. And her feet are slashed up from the dry, hard earth... Even when I'm uncomfortable, sometimes in pain, or just cold... I think, 'Thank God for what I've got.'

Sue Townsend

Feminism is a socialist, anti-family, political movement that encourages women to leave their husbands, kill their children, practice witchcraft, destroy capitalism and become lesbians.

Pat Robertson

Children begin by loving their parents; after a time they

judge them; rarely, if ever, do they forgive them.

Oscar Wilde

When one has love for God, one doesn't feel any physical attraction to wife, children, relatives and friends. One retains only compassion for them.

Ramakrishna

Children have never been very good at listening to their elders, but they have never failed to imitate them.

James A. Baldwin

Treat your kid like a darling for the first five years. For the next five years, scold them. By the time they turn sixteen, treat them like a friend. Your grown up children are your best friends.

Chanakya

I prefer peace. But if trouble must come, let it come in my time, so that my children can live in peace.

Thomas Paine

Little children, you are from God, and have conquered them; for the one who is in you is greater than the one who is in this world.

Jesus Christ

When the human race neglects its weaker members, when the family neglects its weakest one - it's the first blow in a suicidal movement. I see the neglect in cities around the country, in poor white children in West Virginia and Virginia and Kentucky - in the big cities, too, for that matter.

Maya Angelou

It is easier for a father to have children than for children to have a real father.

Pope John XXIII

There are children playing in the streets who could solve some of my top problems in physics, because they have modes of sensory perception that I lost long ago.

J. Robert Oppenheimer

To maintain a joyful family requires much from both the parents and the children. Each member of the family has to become, in a special way, the servant of the others.

Pope John Paul II

Your children need your presence more than your presents.

Jesse Jackson

If we don't stand up for children, then we don't stand for much.

Marian Wright Edelman

Even very young children need to be informed about dying. Explain the concept of death very carefully to your child. This will make threatening him with it much more effective.

P. J. O'Rourke

Children must be considered in a divorce considered valuable pawns in the nasty legal and financial contest that is about to ensue.

P. J. O'Rourke

Peace is one of the most precious gifts God has promised His children.

Joyce Meyer

It is past time for women to take their rightful place, side by side with men, in the rooms where the fates of peoples, where their children's and grandchildren's fates, are decided.

Hillary Clinton

They say that children become men, and men become children. Many generations have grown up, become men, and gone hence.

Sholom Aleichem

Humans are the only animals that have children on purpose with the exception of guppies, who like to eat theirs.

P. J. O'Rourke

If there were no schools to take the children away from home part of the time, the insane asylums would be filled with mothers.

E. W. Howe

Too often we act - ask our schools to be truant officers, our teachers to be truant officers, because we're giving them children who have, you know, they're not ready to learn. And if they're not ready to learn by the third grade, they know they're behind.

Colin Powell

Ah, how many luxuries has the good God prepared for his Jewish children.

Sholom Aleichem

Is adult entertainment killing our children? or is killing our children entertaining our adults?

Marilyn Manson

Just as our ancient ancestors drew animals on cave walls and carved animals from wood and bone, we decorate our homes with animal prints and motifs, give our children stuffed animals to clutch, cartoon animals to watch, animal stories to read.

Diane Ackerman

I'm sometimes scared of everything that has happened to us. We didn't think Desilu Productions would grow so big. We merely wanted to be together and have two children.

Lucille Ball

I was the seventh of nine children. When you come from that far down you have to struggle to survive.

Robert Kennedy

Children, dear and loving children, can alone console a woman for the loss of her beauty.

Honore de Balzac

The well-being and welfare of children should always be our focus.

Todd Tiahrt

Finance, like time, devours its own children.

Honore de Balzac

God is patient with us to become the God's children he wants us to be but you really can see him weeping.

Desmond Tutu

The first half of our lives are ruined by our parents and the second half by our children.

Clarence Darrow

Parents must lead by example. Don't use the cliche; do as I say and not as I do. We are our children's first and most important role models.

Lee Haney

God wants to help us... He loves us... we are His children. But He will not force His help on us at any time. He sees us when we struggle and fight and complain our way through things. And I believe it breaks His heart, when all we have to do is ask Him for help.

Joyce Meyer

I hope I am remembered by my children as a good father.

Orson Scott Card

There are still thousands of people dying every year in Laos, mostly children and farmers, from unexploded anti-personnel ordnance that the U.S. simply saturated much of the land with, especially in the Plain of Jars. There actually is a British engineering team trying to remove some of these things, which are much worse than land mines.

Noam Chomsky

Buildings, too, are children of Earth and Sun.

Frank Lloyd Wright

I saw as a teacher how, if you take that spark of learning that those children have, and you ignite it, you can take a child from any background to a lifetime of creativity and accomplishment.

Paul Wellstone

I would say the most satisfying thing actually is watching my three children each pick up on their own interests and work many more hours per week than most people that have jobs at trying to intelligently give away that money in fields that they particularly care about.

Warren Buffett

Women have always been courageous... They are always fearless when protecting their children and in the last century they have been fearless in the fight for their rights.

Isabel Allende

If you read 'Lord of the Rings' and dismiss it as a lie because it has orcs and elves, you're missing the whole point of the story. If children don't have to be concerned about strangers because there's no such thing as a Big Bad Wolf dressed like Granny, you're missing the point.

Doug TenNapel

Woman must have her freedom, the fundamental freedom of choosing whether or not she will be a mother and how many children she will have. Regardless of what man's attitude may be, that problem is hers - and before it can be his, it is hers alone.

Margaret Sanger

Children show scars like medals. Lovers use them as secrets to reveal. A scar is what happens when the word is made flesh.

Leonard Cohen

I believe that parents need to make nutrition education a priority in their home environment. It's crucial for good health and longevity to instill in your children sound eating habits from an early age.

Cat Cora

Children show me in their playful smiles the divine in everyone. This simple goodness shines straight from their hearts and only asks to be loved.

Michael Jackson

Child abuse and neglect offend the basic values of our state. We have a responsibility to provide safe settings for at-risk children and facilitate permanent placement for children who cannot return home.

Matt Blunt

Let parents bequeath to their children not riches, but the spirit of reverence.

Plato

I cannot think that we are useless or God would not have created us. There is one God looking down on us all. We are all the children of one God. The sun, the darkness, the winds are all listening to what we have to say.

Geronimo

Suppose that every prospective parent in the world stopped having children naturally, and instead produced clones of themselves. What would the world be like in another 20 or 30 years? The answer is: much like today. Cloning would only copy the genetic aspects of people who are already here.

Nathan Myhrvold

And also I didn't want my future to be just sitting in a room and be imprisoned in my four walls and just cooking and giving birth to children. I didn't want to see my life in that way.

Malala Yousafzai

In the family, in interpersonal relationships, even in friendship, faith is tremendously important. If you have a partner who you believe is a good person, then it is your duty to have faith in them until the end, despite the fact that they might have done some bad things. And you have to support and believe in your children.

Greg Graffin

The leading cause of death for girls 15 to 19 worldwide is not accident or violence or disease; it is complications from pregnancy. Girls under 15 are up to five times as likely to die while having children than are women in their 20s, and their babies are more likely to die as well.

Nancy Gibbs

When we were children, we used to think that when we were grown-up we would no longer be vulnerable. But to grow up is to accept vulnerability... To be alive is to be vulnerable.

Madeleine L'Engle

Children are completely egoistic; they feel their needs intensely and strive ruthlessly to satisfy them.

Sigmund Freud

We are a nation of immigrants. We are the children and grandchildren and great-grandchildren of the ones who wanted a better life, the driven ones, the ones who woke up at night hearing that voice telling them that life in that place called America could be better.

Mitt Romney

Everything that I love is behind those gates. We have elephants, and giraffes, and crocodiles, and every kind of tigers and lions. And - and we have bus loads of kids, who don't get to see those things. They come up sick children, and enjoy it.

Michael Jackson

Remember that children, marriages, and flower gardens reflect the kind of care they get.

H. Jackson Brown, Jr.

When families are strong and stable, so are children - showing higher levels of wellbeing and more positive outcomes. But when things go wrong - either through family breakdown or a damaged parental relationship - the impact on a child's later life can be devastating.

Iain Duncan Smith

I came home every Friday afternoon, riding the six miles on the back of a big mule. I spent Saturday and Sunday washing and ironing and cooking for the children and went back to my country school on Sunday afternoon.

Ida B. Wells

The use of the atomic bomb, with its indiscriminate killing of women and children, revolts my soul.

Herbert Hoover

Reading should not be presented to children as a chore, a duty. It should be offered as a gift.

Kate DiCamillo

It's more pressure on women to - if they marry or partner with someone, to partner with the right person. Because you cannot have a full career and a full life at home with your children if you are also doing all of the housework and child care.

Sheryl Sandberg

That's one of the biggest losses, I think, to African American families, is that people, once they left, they turned away from the South. They didn't look back, and they often didn't tell their children about it. They didn't want to talk about it. It was too painful, what they'd gone through and the caste system of the South, which was Jim Crow.

Isabel Wilkerson

You can learn many things from children. How much patience you have, for instance.

Franklin P. Jones

For just a few dollars a dose, vaccines save lives and help reduce poverty. Unlike medical treatment, they provide a lifetime of protection from deadly and debilitating disease. They are safe and effective. They cut healthcare and treatment costs, reduce the number of hospital visits, and ensure healthier children, families and communities.

Seth Berkley

How paramount the future is to the present when one is surrounded by children.

Charles Darwin

Children require guidance and sympathy far more than instruction.

Anne Sullivan

There's no reason why children in inner cities or rural areas do not receive the same quality education or opportunities as those in suburbs or wealthy neighborhoods. If we truly believe in giving all citizens a chance to pursue happiness and pursue their goals, then we cannot continue to marginalize entire groups of people.

Al Sharpton

The pursuit of truth and beauty is a sphere of activity in which we are permitted to remain children all our lives.

Albert Einstein

It took a lot of blood, sweat and tears to get to where we are today, but we have just begun. Today we begin in earnest the work of making sure that the world we leave our children is just a little bit better than the one we inhabit today.

Barack Obama

War may sometimes be a necessary evil. But no matter how necessary, it is always an evil, never a good. We will not learn how to live together in peace by killing each other's children.

Jimmy Carter

Our redemption through the suffering of Christ is that deeper love within us which not only frees us from slavery to sin, but also secures for us the true liberty of the children of God, in order that we might do all things out of love rather than out of fear - love for him that has shown us such grace that no greater can be found.

Peter Abelard

School is where children spend most of their time, and it is where we lay the foundation for healthy habits. That's why

New Jersey is the first state to adopt a comprehensive school nutrition policy that bans candy, soda, and other junk food.

Richard J. Codey

The focus of tolerance education is to deal with the concept of equality and fairness. We need to establish confidence with children that there is more goodness than horror in this world.

Morris Dees

Let children read whatever they want and then talk about it with them. If parents and kids can talk together, we won't have as much censorship because we won't have as much fear.

Judy Blume

We cannot and will not ban the creation of violent video games. But, we can prevent the distribution of these disturbing games to children, where their effects can be negative.

Herb Kohl

No one ever died from sleeping in an unmade bed. I have known mothers who remake the bed after their children do it because there is wrinkle in the spread or the blanket is on crooked. This is sick.

Erma Bombeck

Happiness is an imaginary condition, formerly attributed by the living to the dead, now usually attributed by adults to children, and by children to adults.

Thomas Szasz

A high-speed connection is no more an essential civil right than 3G cell phone service or a Netflix account. Increasing competition and restoring academic excellence in abysmal public schools is far more of an imperative to minority children than handing them iPads.

Michelle Malkin

Children make your life important.

Erma Bombeck

With your own children, you love them immediately - and

with grandchildren, it's exactly the same.

Kevin Whately

By nature, I'm a very positive person, and because I'm happy in myself, and in my life, and I've got a great husband, and beautiful children, and I have a job that I love that calls for a certain amount of emotional expression, I get to realise a lot of my dreams and aspirations.

Kate Winslet

I'm a hopeless romantic. I love love. My middle name is Love. Valentine's Day is my favorite holiday. I want to have a family and children. I am a sucker for every romantic comedy that comes out.

Jennifer Love Hewitt

To my young friends out there: Life can be great, but not when you can't see it. So, open your eyes to life: to see it in the vivid colors that God gave us as a precious gift to His children, to enjoy life to the fullest, and to make it count. Say yes to your life.

Nancy Reagan

Teach love, generosity, good manners and some of that will drift from the classroom to the home and who knows, the children will be educating the parents.

Roger Moore

If my books can help children become readers, then I feel I have accomplished something important.

Roald Dahl

We owe it to ourselves and to the next generation to conserve the environment so that we can bequeath our children a sustainable world that benefits all.

Wangari Maathai

Men fear death as children fear to go in the dark; and as that natural fear in children is increased by tales, so is the other.

Francis Bacon

I never thought I'd have children; I never thought I'd be in love, I never thought I'd meet the right person. Having come from a broken home - you kind of accept that certain things feel like a fairy tale, and you just don't look for them.

Angelina Jolie

I find that the only way to make my characters really interesting to children is to exaggerate all their good or bad qualities, and so if a person is nasty or bad or cruel, you make them very nasty, very bad, very cruel. If they are ugly, you make them extremely ugly. That, I think, is fun and makes an impact.

Roald Dahl

Children tease each other because you're short or you're tall or you're a redhead or because you're ugly or because you're smart or because you're dumb or all kinds of differences and as parents we have to deal with that and strengthen our children to be comfortable with themselves and also to show empathy and acceptance towards others.

Heather Wilson

The children have been a wonderful gift to me, and I'm thankful to have once again seen our world through their eyes. They restore my faith in the family's future.

Jackie Kennedy

We have come to a turning point in the road. If we turn to the right mayhap our children and our children's children will go that way; but if we turn to the left, generations yet unborn will curse our names for having been unfaithful to God and to His Word.

Charles Spurgeon

A woman caring for her children; a woman striving to excel in the private sector; a woman partnering with her neighbors to make their street safer; a woman running for office to improve her country - they all have something to offer, and the more our societies empower women, the more we receive in return.

Queen Rania of Jordan

The issue of equal rights for lesbian, gay, bisexual and transgender individuals has vexed politicians for decades. I have my own cloudy history with the issue, having supported a law in Mississippi that made it illegal for LGBT couples to adopt children. I believed at the time this was a principled position based on my faith.

Ronnie Musgrove

If it is right for men to fight for their freedom, and God knows what the human race would be like today if men had not, since time began, fought for their freedom, then it is right for women to fight for their freedom and the freedom of the children they bear.

Emmeline Pankhurst

Human relationships used to be easy: you had friends, boy- or girlfriends, parents, children, and landlords. Now, thanks to social media, it's all gone sideways.

Susan Orlean

The soul is healed by being with children.

Fyodor Dostoevsky

I love my children and I love my wife with all my heart. And I would die, die gladly, if that would make a better life for them.

Medgar Evers

We have to bring children into a new relationship to food that connects them to culture and agriculture.

Alice Waters

But I do believe that a woman's truest place is in a home, with a husband and with children, and with large freedom, pecuniary freedom, personal freedom, and the right to vote.

Lucy Stone

In Georgia where children work day and night in the cotton mills they have just passed a bill to protect song birds. What about the little children from whom all song is gone?

Mary Harris Jones

I want to walk into a room, be it a hospital for the dying or a hospital for the sick children, and feel that I am needed. I want to do, not just to be.

Princess Diana

The most sophisticated people I know - inside they are all children.

Jim Henson

Steve Jobs, Bill Gates and Mark Zuckerberg didn't finish college. Too much emphasis is placed on formal education - I told my children not to worry about their grades but to enjoy learning.

Nassim Nicholas Taleb

Our youth deserve the opportunity to complete their high school and college education, free of early parenthood. Their future children deserve the opportunity to grow up in financially and emotionally stable homes. Our communities benefit from healthy, productive, well-prepared young people.

Jane Fonda

I find it interesting that 16-year-olds are having plastic surgery. People in their 40s used to think, 'I'm aging, I have to do something about it.' Now children are deciding they don't like the way they look.

Jane Seymour

Seems like God don't see fit to give the black man nothing but dreams - but He did give us children to make them dreams seem worthwhile.

Lorraine Hansberry

When you go somewhere like Kenya and you see how the children don't have pencils and pens, and all of these things are considered luxuries, and what a privilege they see education as and how hungry they are to learn, I wanted to give my brother and sister long lectures. That definitely stayed with me.

Naomie Harris

But to the slave mother New Year's day comes laden with peculiar sorrows. She sits on her cold cabin floor, watching the children who may all be torn from her the next morning; and often does she wish that she and they might die before the day dawns.

Harriet Ann Jacobs

Children are not casual guests in our home. They have been loaned to us temporarily for the purpose of loving them and instilling a foundation of values on which their future lives will be built.

James Dobson

Libraries allow children to ask questions about the world and find the answers. And the wonderful thing is that once a child learns to use a library, the doors to learning are always open.

Laura Bush

Children learn to smile from their parents.

Shinichi Suzuki

I come from that society and there is a common thread, specifically family values - the idea that you do anything for your family, and the unconditional love for one's children.

Ednita Nazario

It is up to us to live up to the legacy that was left for us, and to leave a legacy that is worthy of our children and of future generations.

Christine Gregoire

We are all in the business of sales. Teachers sell students on learning, parents sell their children on making good grades and behaving, and traditional salesmen sell their products.

Dave Ramsey

Every comedian is furious. Age makes me angry. I'm
unhappy at not being able to open packages anymore. I'm
angry that libraries have gone. I hate children on planes.
I'm very shallow, so they tend to be little things. To be
honest, I think I was probably angry the day I was born,
you know, about diapers or something.

Joan Rivers

I am poor and naked, but I am the chief of the nation. We
do not want riches but we do want to train our children
right. Riches would do us no good. We could not take them
with us to the other world. We do not want riches. We want
peace and love.

Red Cloud

The future which we hold in trust for our own children will
be shaped by our fairness to other people's children.

Marian Wright Edelman

What is sad for women of my generation is that they
weren't supposed to work if they had families. What were

they going to do when the children are grown - watch the raindrops coming down the window pane?

Jackie Kennedy

We can either continue to collectively stand on the sidelines and debate what is causing autism and if it is an epidemic or we can get on the field and start addressing the real problem - a generation of children with autism. We are not focusing enough on prevention, treatments and support services.

Jenny McCarthy

Though the Jazz Age continued it became less and less an affair of youth. The sequel was like a children's party taken over by the elders.

F. Scott Fitzgerald

If you ask 99.9 percent of parents who have children with autism if we'd rather have the measles versus autism, we'd sign up for the measles.

Jenny McCarthy

No one ever said that fighting the war against terrorism and defending our homeland would be easy. So let's support our troops, law enforcement workers, and our mission to keep our nation and our children safe in the days and years to come.

Judy Biggert

Children say that people are hung sometimes for speaking the truth.

Joan of Arc

Children love and want to be loved and they very much prefer the joy of accomplishment to the triumph of hateful failure. Do not mistake a child for his symptom.

Erik Erikson

I always knew I wanted to have children. When I met my husband, Rande, I thought, 'This is the guy.' When you are getting ready to become a mom, being in love with someone just isn't enough. You need to think about whether he would be a good parent and raise your children with similar beliefs.

Cindy Crawford

I'm sorry, it's true. Having children really changes your view on these things. We're born, we live for a brief instant, and we die. It's been happening for a long time. Technology is not changing it much - if at all.

Steve Jobs

A true conservationist is a man who knows that the world is not given by his fathers, but borrowed from his children.

John James Audubon

When faced with a challenge, happy families, like happy people, just add a new chapter to their life story that shows them overcoming the hardship. This skill is particularly important for children, whose identity tends to get locked in during adolescence.

Bruce Feiler

The malaria parasite has been killing children and sapping the strength of whole populations for tens of thousands of years. It is impossible to calculate the harm malaria has done to the world.

Bill Gates

A good mother remembers to serve fruit at breakfast, is always cheerful and never yells, manages not to project her own neuroses and inadequacies onto her children, is an active and beloved community volunteer. She remembers to make play dates, her children's clothes fit, she does art projects with them and enjoys all their games.

Ayelet Waldman

If all the rich and all of the church people should send their children to the public schools they would feel bound to concentrate their money on improving these schools until they met the highest ideals.

Susan B. Anthony

I have found the best way to give advice to your children is to find out what they want and then advise them to do it.

Harry S Truman

Schools connect children to their communities. Jobs connect adults to their societies. Persons with autism deserve to walk the same path.

Ban Ki-moon

Parents are working more than ever before and unable to monitor what kids are eating at home, and schools are selling astronomical amounts of junk food in order to supplement shrinking budgets. It's a ticking time bomb, and America's children are exploding.

Lisa Ling

We believed in our idea - a family park where parents and children could have fun- together.

Walt Disney

Raising children is an uncertain thing; success is reached only after a life of battle and worry.

Democritus

Yes sir, I am a tortured man for all seasons, as they say, and I have powerful friends in high places. Birds sing where I walk, and children smile when they see me coming.

Hunter S. Thompson

One of the many interesting and surprising experiences of

the beginner in child analysis is to find in even very young children a capacity for insight which is often far greater than that of adults.

Melanie Klein

I remember one time when all the nuns in my Catholic grade school got around in a semicircle, me and Mom in the middle, and they said, 'Mrs. Farley, the children at school are laughing at Christopher, not with him.' I thought, 'Who cares? As long as they're laughing.'

Chris Farley

A girl child who is even a little bit educated is more conscious of family planning, health care and, in turn, her children's own education.

Azim Premji

All of us have moments in our lives that test our courage. Taking children into a house with a white carpet is one of them.

Erma Bombeck

If you are a parent, you have probably already realized that your children are always watching what you do. And just as children watch their parents and emulate their behavior, so do employees who are watching their bosses.

John C. Maxwell

What is success? It is a toy balloon among children armed with pins.

Gene Fowler

Everybody knows how to raise children, except the people who have them.

P. J. O'Rourke

We are apt to forget that children watch examples better than they listen to preaching.

Roy L. Smith

The production of children, the nurture of those born, and the daily life of men, of these matters woman is visibly the cause.

Guru Nanak

The lack of access to proper nutrition is not only fueling obesity, it is leading to food insecurity and hunger among our children.

Tom Vilsack

The United Nations Children's Fund reports that more than 18 million children worldwide have lost both parents to the ravages of AIDS, starvation, war or natural disasters.

Foster Friess

There are no adequate substitutes for father, mother, and children bound together in a loving commitment to nurture and protect. No government, no matter how well-intentioned, can take the place of the family in the scheme of things.

Gerald R. Ford

My parents were children during the Great Depression of the 1930s, and it scarred them. Especially my father, who saw destitution in his Brooklyn, New York neighborhood; adults standing in so called 'bread lines,' children begging in the streets.

Bill O'Reilly

Perhaps my children will one day pledge their loyalty to the
Republican Party. Or perhaps they'll dismiss my liberalism
as mild pap, and become anarchists. Either way may well
be a reaction to my manipulation, my values. We are all the
product of the indoctrination we received at the hands of
our parents, even when we are repudiating that ideology.

Ayelet Waldman

Children used to get bullied at school. Now they go home,
and that's where the problem starts - because they sit on
their phones all night, thinking about who's 'liked' a photo
of them, who hates them, who loves them. They don't know
what's real and what's not, editing their lives constantly to
fit other people's views.

Jessie J

As a father, I believe that involving children in sports at a
young age is generally, a wise proposition. I believe that
healthy competition is... well... healthy; that sporting events
foster a spirit of teamwork that far surpasses the events
themselves; and that active participation keeps children
moving and is good for their self-esteem.

Naveen Jain

Sometimes even the greatest joys bring challenge, and children with special needs inspire a very, very special love.

Sarah Palin

If you bungle raising your children, I don't think whatever else you do matters very much.

Jackie Kennedy

An arts education helps build academic skills and increase academic performance, while also providing alternative opportunities to reward the skills of children who learn differently.

Gavin Newsom

Nobody can do for little children what grandparents do. Grandparents sort of sprinkle stardust over the lives of little children.

Alex Haley

Children are our most valuable natural resource.

Herbert Hoover

As long as there are people in education making excuses for failure, cursing future generations with a culture of low expectations, denying children access to the best that has been thought and written, because Nemo and the Mister Men are more relevant, the battle needs to be joined.

Michael Gove

Children have to be educated, but they have also to be left to educate themselves.

Ernest Dimnet

Get FREE Kindle Books Every Week,

Delivered by Email!

Click Here or go to quoteoctopus.com to get your free books!

www.ingramcontent.com/pod-product-compliance
Lightning Source LLC
Chambersburg PA
CBHW070636290526
45790CB00001B/107